LEVELING
THE ICE

LEVELING THE ICE

CONFRONTING RACISM

IN HOCKEY

STEVEN SANDOR

BEACON PRESS | BOSTON

BEACON PRESS
Boston, Massachusetts
www.beacon.org

Beacon Press books
are published under the auspices of
the Unitarian Universalist Association of Congregations.

28 27 26 25   8 7 6 5 4 3 2 1

This book is printed on acid-free paper that meets the uncoated paper ANSI/
NISO specifications for permanence as revised in 1992.

Text design by BookMatters

*Library of Congress Cataloguing-in-Publication Data
is available for this title.*

Hardcover ISBN: 978-0-8070-2046-3
E-book ISBN: 978-0-8070-2045-6
Audiobook: 978-0-8070-2228-3

The authorized representative in the EU for product safety and compliance is
Easy Access System Europe 16879218, Mustamäe tee 50, 10621 Tallinn, Estonia:
http://beacon.org/eu-contact

For Nico and Tate:
Sports offer the toughest lessons of all.
I am proud of you—and I believe you.

CONTENTS

INTRODUCTION

HOCKEY CULTURE. There are no written rules, yet everyone on or off the ice follows them. The culture exists on the rinks where kids are learning to skate, all the way up to National Hockey League (NHL) arenas. The culture is what keeps hockey isolated from the rest of the sporting world. It is celebrated across Canada and makes hockey the outlier of the so-called Big Four leagues in the United States.

How to change something without a code, without a set of rules, that silently governs hockey, players, coaches, managers, and officials?

In order to talk about racism in hockey, we have to address the culture that allows it to continue.

For most of my nearly three decades of being involved in hockey—whether it is covering the sport, or in my time working as the publications coordinator for an NHL team—I haven't been an outspoken critic of the culture.

I've been part of the culture.

I'm part of the old-school hockey establishment. As a white male hockey writer, I was under contract to the Edmonton Oilers from 1998 till the 2004 lockout. If you are of a certain age, you may remember the game programs that you could buy for a few bucks, that had a few articles and the lineups of the teams taking the ice that night. You'd hear the hawker—"get yer pro-grammms, just five bucks!"—as you navigated your way toward your seats, surrounded by the comforting smells of hot dogs and popcorn. I was in charge of producing those programs. I edited the stories, wrote some of the pieces, sourced the photos, signed off on the covers.

Despite the changes in technology, I see myself reflected in NHL press boxes every night. We show up to the arena a couple of hours before face-off, get the pregame media meal, get seconds of the pregame media meal, and spend the next few hours judging the exploits of star athletes.

Despite being a dad in a mixed-race family, I've often treated issues of race as something I need to tiptoe around. But as I got more and more involved in youth sports, and talked at length with elite BIPOC hockey players, I saw that there was no need to be polite when it comes to the issues of race and diversity, and the need for equity in the games that we play. There were times in the past couple of years that some of my media colleagues wondered why I was stirring up the hornet's nest when I told them I was working on a book about racism in hockey. To them, there was no problem—or it wasn't part of our job to write about these kinds of stories.

What made this so hypocritical on my part is my strong belief that sport is one of the most political things that we do. When people ask media to "stick to sports," it's clear that they've totally missed the point.

From the gladiators in Roman arenas, to the early days of Association Football in England, sport has always had a political aim. Why do we have national anthems before the games? Why is it that the world comes to a standstill to see which country wins the World Cup or earns the most Olympic medals? Why would Communist nations work so hard to cheat the system if there wasn't great political value to having more gold medals than anyone else?

The link between sports and politics has always been clear to me. But why did it take me so long to make that connection between hockey and race? And why do so many of my colleagues fail to see it?

Hockey has so many great stories to tell, but at times there's an unwritten code between media, teams, and players that we can't do more than simply write about who won, who scored, and who's in a slump. Talking about racism in hockey puts the game's predominantly white old guard under the microscope. We live in a world where liking the "right" social media posts is often seen as enough. As long as you make it look good, you don't have to worry about actually following through.

I don't think the old guard is some sort of evil cabal; we're just desperately out of touch. Reporting on hockey is a privilege. We get to go to the arena regularly, many travel across North America with the teams, and we can get caught within our own small world. We hear the platitudes from the leaders of the game, and we say, "That's a really big step" and don't really question why the pace of change in the game is so slow.

The rise of social media and the instant soundbite has made players and team public relations staff more and more wary about what they say. Teams stream news conferences and dressing room interviews on their websites—and that allows them to take control of the message. On many nights, the postgame press conferences have become so safe, so mundane, that we've created a series of Groundhog Days where the scores and standings might change, but the storylines remain rigid.

Meanwhile, the NHL, USA Hockey, and Hockey Canada have begun speaking loudly about the need to diversify the game. That message is also coming from major junior hockey leagues and minor-hockey organizations. But saying you want to do a thing is a lot different than, well, actually doing the thing. Hockey rinks across Canada and the United States are still overwhelmingly white and don't reflect the cultural mosaic of North America. And that problem goes all the way down to the grassroots.

So while the NHL has TV deals worth hundreds of millions with ESPN, TNT in the United States, and north of a billion with the Rogers cable empire in Canada, and teams increasing their worth every season, the number of kids playing the game is shrinking in North America.

Hockey Canada's 2022–23 annual report showed that registration numbers were rebounding as the world recovers from pandemic slow-downs and lockdowns. It showed a total of 550,137 registered players for the reporting period. That's still about 200,000 fewer registered players than there were a decade ago. In the United States, there were 556,186 registered players, according to USA Hockey. Those numbers are up over the previous season, but still below where they were before the pandemic. In 2018–19, there were more than 567,000 registered players in America. There is one big asterisk that we need to slap onto USA Hockey's registra-tion stats: it's that the biggest drop in registrations is among players aged six and under. That means fewer parents are willing to start their kids in organized hockey at a young age.

When I started writing this book, I imagined it was going to be a lot more hopeful than it turned out to be. I really wanted to believe that this sport was living up to its promises that it would be more inclusive. But as I write this in 2023–24, lip service outstrips real and meaningful action by a long shot. Saddest of all was when I would talk to athletes of color about the other stories I'd heard, the reaction was similar—it was "It's good to see that you're angry about it, but this doesn't surprise us. We've seen it all."

I am thankful to all those who agreed to be interviewed for this book, as well as those who sent messages of support but declined my requests. Being interviewed is a choice that a person makes, and we need to respect a person's right to say no.

On top of that, there were many teams that responded positively to my interview requests. But there were others that didn't respond at all, not even to send a "no thanks" message as a reply. The NHL says it wants to change the game, but from my experience working on this book, there are still NHL clubs out there that don't want to engage in this topic outside of theme nights and Instagram posts.

But we need to have these uncomfortable conversations, especially people like me, white male members of the hockey establishment and fans. And once we've had the uncomfortable discussions, we have to follow them with concrete actions. We need better, mixed representation in our national sporting organizations. We need better, mixed representation in our local hockey associations. And we need to confront and speak against any sort of racism we witness as we watch a game. Any game.

And those actions will lead to more kids picking up sticks and lacing up skates. Because there's two words that should inspire any kid, no matter their background or economic standing.

Game On.

LEVELING
THE ICE

ONE

THE WAY FORWARD

KIM DAVIS'S SON was at a private all-boys school in Connecticut. Part of the phys ed requirement was for all students to play hockey.

Her son immediately took to the game. He already knew how to skate and was an all-around great athlete. "He was a natural. He enjoyed it," Davis recalled.

But during a game, a parent uttered the N-word in his direction. And at that moment, curriculum be damned, he decided that hockey wasn't for him. At age eleven, he quit playing a game he had fallen in love with just a short time earlier.

"He hung up his skates and that was the end of it," said Davis. "He was not mad, he was disgusted. He couldn't believe this was going on in the sport, with kids on the ice."

Fast-forward two decades. The woman who was a hockey mom for a fleeting time is now one of the most important people in the game. In 2018, the National Hockey League hired Davis to become its executive vice president, in charge of growth and diversity initiatives. At the end of a lengthy interview, I asked her if, years ago, she could have ever imagined she'd become one of the most impactful figures in a game that's long been branded a white sport. She answered with the story about her son's short experience with the game.

"I always think hockey missed out on someone who potentially could have gone far in the sport," she said. "And here I am, twenty years later, in a movement to improve the [hockey] culture."

Davis's hiring represented a sea change for the game of hockey. Davis had previously been a big-time consultant to major corporations in the fields of corporate responsibility and inclusive practices. She helped international tennis legend Billie Jean King found her philanthropic foundation. And before that, she was part of the executive committee at JPMorgan Chase in charge of the firm's charitable and civic engagement initiatives. She was also a senior managing director at Teneo, a company that consults CEOs of major companies around the world.

Make no mistake—hockey represents Davis's largest challenge. Fixing Wall Street has nothing on taking on hockey's culture from within.

During her first year on the job, she visited twenty-eight NHL cities as well as Seattle, which was coming into the league via expansion. And she heard the same message over and over.

"Through all of that, I would constantly hear in those communities, from folks of color, that they love the sport, but they never felt like it loved them," said Davis. "Therefore, they would actually pretend to their friends that they didn't like hockey. They felt like such outsiders."

It's not hard to see why. In 2023, *Bostonia*, the alumni magazine of Boston University, published a profile of former Boston University Terrier player Mike Grier, who was recently named the general manager of the San Jose Sharks—and the first Black man to ever take the helm of an NHL club. It stated that, when Grier was hired, just 4.8 percent of the NHL's players were BIPOC—Black, Indigenous, and People of Color.[1]

The size of an NHL roster is between twenty and twenty-three players, depending on how each club manages the salary cap. Some teams carry fewer players because they've already spent to the limit. That percentage suggests that only one out of every twenty players isn't white. So, it works out to maybe an average of a little better than 1 BIPOC player per team.

Of the thirty-two players selected in the first round of the 2023 NHL Draft, all were white. Because most newly selected prospects aren't ready for the NHL, even the first-rounders, they remain with their NCAA, junior, or international clubs. Of the thirty-two, four started the season in the Kontinental Hockey League—in Russia, a country that's been censured by the United States and Canada for its invasion of Ukraine. As of the writing of this book, the International Ice Hockey Federation does not allow Russian national teams to play in its competitions, like the Worlds and World Junior Championships.

In 2024, though, three players of color—Cayden Lindstrom, Tij Iginla (son of NHL Hall of Famer Jarome Iginla), and Zayne Parekh—were taken in the top ten of the draft. But how the draft goes is a measure of how well the grassroots are doing when it comes to not only welcoming a diverse array of talent but nurturing them to be their best.

Obviously, the draft is based on merit. Sports are supposed to be a results-oriented meritocracy. The question is, why isn't the talent pool diversifying at a faster pace? Why aren't there more players of color evolving into legitimate prospects?

Matt Dumba, a defenseman of Filipino heritage, spoke about how, well, *white* the average NHL game feels. Dumba spoke to me at length while he was in the final year of a five-year contract with the Minnesota Wild, before he signed a one-year deal with the Arizona Coyotes before the 2023–24 season. He was dealt to the Tampa Bay Lightning at the 2024 trade deadline, and then signed with the Dallas Stars in July 2024.

"I talk to my friends who come to games, even at the National Hockey League level, and they feel that they're alienated at the game," said Dumba. "They stick out, and it's not the most welcoming environment. It's a white game, if I want to be so bold about it. That's just a matter of fact. It's exactly what we're trying to change."

Darnell Nurse, a Black defenseman with the Edmonton Oilers, was frank in his assessment of what it's like to grow up in Canada as a non-white player.

"Hockey has been Canada's game for so many years," he said. "And as a country, we like to brag about how diverse we are and how inclusive we are as a people and as a country. Hockey hasn't had the same effect, the same look. You look around hockey arenas, they don't have lots of Black players, players of Asian descent, Aboriginal players. It doesn't have that feel—there are a lot of white players who play hockey."

These stark numbers actually represent a bold improvement in the NHL. A generation ago, a player of color was a rarity in the league. But the NHL, and hockey as a whole, have a long way to go. The math is simple:

the only way to have more players of color taken in the early rounds of the draft, or making it to NHL rosters, is by having more BIPOC kids enter hockey programs. From the rinks in St. Paul, Minnesota, to St. Paul, Alberta, everywhere needs to become more diverse.

Several times during our interview, Davis referred to the NHL as the "North Star" of the sport. It's the world's best and most-recognized league. What happens in the NHL affects minor-hockey players and coaches not only in North America but in the pockets of Europe where the game is strong.

Davis's raison d'être is simple. This is what she's brought from Wall Street to the NHL's headquarters in Midtown Manhattan: If sporting organizations keep looking at diversity as a charitable endeavor, it won't work. But if they look at it through the cold eyes of economics, then the movement will gain traction.

"When I would talk to executives at the clubs, they would always refer to under-indexed audiences and underrepresented groups through a charitable lens, not a growth lens," Davis said. "They would be talking about *helping* and not understanding that, with demographic shifts happening across North America, we were the ones that needed the help.

"We have to get our fair share of new audiences and fans-in-waiting, and they are multicultural, younger, and tech-savvy—and female. And if we didn't lean into that, we were going to lose, we weren't going to win in the marketplace. What I have seen over these now-six years is a reframing and a reawakening of stakeholders at every level in the organization. They're embracing this idea that under-indexed audiences are our future through growth. This is *not* a charitable endeavor."

The numbers show that the NHL needs to grow in new areas because the traditional areas of reach are tapped out.

The 2022–23 season marked the NHL's first with TNT as a broadcast partner, and playoff games earned a little under a million viewers each on that network, according to parent company Warner Bros. Discovery Sports. The 2023 Stanley Cup final between the Vegas Golden Knights and Florida Panthers drew about 1.2 million viewers per game on ESPN.[2] That's a decline of almost half from the 2022 final, which saw the Colorado Avalanche beat the Tampa Bay Lightning. In 2024, the Edmonton Oilers/Florida Panthers Stanley Cup final, broadcast by ESPN/ABC in the United States, achieved ratings 15–20 percent higher than the 2023 final, but didn't come close to the 2022 numbers.

Go back to 2014, and NBC reported viewerships of better than four million per game for the Cup final between the Los Angeles Kings and New York Rangers. Two major-market teams, for sure—but there's no doubt the numbers have been in serious decline over the last decade. In 2023–24, numbers showed some improvement on TNT and ESPN, but they have a long way to go.

And every Canadian is obsessed with hockey, right? The global stereotype is that all Canadians ever watch or talk about is hockey—but the reality is the most popular sport in my home country, in terms of viewership, is American football. Canadians love it.

Canadians are also obsessed with the Toronto Blue Jays. As the only Canadian club playing top-flight baseball, the Jays dominate national headlines. According to Numeris, Canada's radio and television monitoring giant, the 2022 Stanley Cup final between the Colorado Avalanche and Tampa Bay Lightning drew about 1.2 million viewers per game. Canada's population is, at the time of writing, about 41 million, a little better than an eighth of America's. So, to get an apples-to-apples comparison, multiply the Canadian numbers by eight to get a comparable US TV rating.

In 2011, when the Vancouver Canucks lost to the Boston Bruins in a thrilling seven-game Cup final, CBC reported average ratings of better than 5.5 million viewers for Game 2 of that seven-game series. From 5.5 million to 1.2 million in a little over a decade—if the NHL was a scripted show, the showrunners would be killing off characters en masse to jump-start viewership.

Blue Jays regular-season games, when the team is in the pennant race, can touch a million viewers each. And according to a postgame, breast-beating press release from The Sports Network (known simply as TSN in Canada), Super Bowl LVIII was an even bigger media bonanza than the release of a new Taylor Swift single. An estimated 50 percent of Canada's population tuned in to at least some portion of the game. Even *Americans* don't love American football as much as Canadians do.

The simple truth is, the NHL's marquee event doesn't come close to the NFL's, and is only slightly better than when the Jays are having a good regular season.

Numeris stopped making TV ratings public in late 2022. The industry is moving to be more secretive about numbers as websites and streaming services like YouTube have fractured viewership. Today, it's relatively simple: If the viewership numbers are good, the network will do a victory lap and tell you about it—like those Super Bowl ratings. If the numbers aren't strong, you'll never hear about them.

The future is even cloudier. While the NHL currently has ESPN (Disney) and TNT (Warner Bros.) deals in the United States, and a deal with telecommunications giant Rogers (who also own the Toronto Blue Jays) in Canada, will the rights fees be the same in years to come? In April 2025, Rogers signed an $11 billion (Canadian currency) deal to be the national broadcaster of NHL games until 2038. It's a big gamble.

Just before Christmas 2023, the NHL and the Diamond Sports Group came to an agreement that sort of saved eleven local TV deals. Diamond's eleven regional networks would limp to the end of the 2023–24 season, with "a reduction in rights payments for some teams."[3] Just before the 2024–25 season, a last-second deal was worked out to save local broadcasts for the Detroit Red Wings, Anaheim Ducks, Columbus Blue Jackets, Carolina Hurricanes, Minnesota Wild, Nashville Predators, and Tampa Bay Lightning, while rights-sharing agreements were reached in Los Angeles and St. Louis for the Kings and Blues, respectively. While some are fringe hockey markets, there were two teams from America's second-largest metro area—Los Angeles. Also represented were the hockey-mad Twin Cities and the place we know as "Hockeytown," Detroit. So, even in American hockey strongholds, local broadcasts suffer.

Outside of the National Football League, which is a juggernaut, sports leagues across North America have to count every fan they earn, and retain, in a time of fractured media and reduced attention spans.

"How do we change hockey's spine?" said Davis. "How do we make sure this culture work trickles down from the very top? If we are the North Star, it is our responsibility to make sure the entire ecosystem benefits from what we can do both financially and what we can do as a moral imperative to make the game better."

Davis is not alone. In hockey, the tone of the debate about race and inclusion has changed over the past five years. Hockey has shifted from "do we have a race problem?" to "yes, we do, and we need to address it." That's not to say that all the professional leagues and grassroots have accepted what has always been right in front of their eyes to be true. But both USA Hockey and Hockey Canada have brought in thought leaders who are giving the organizations new road maps to follow.

Stephanie Jackson was hired as USA Hockey's director of diversity and inclusion in 2019, coming to the national organization from Nike. Why make the jump? "USA Hockey is a nonprofit and it's connected to the Olympic movement," said Jackson. "What better way to express my love of sport than one that shows your love of the country?"

And she said USA Hockey recognized it "had to match the speed of how fast communities in hockey were changing."

Growing up in a military family that jumped from country to country, Jackson had the view that hockey was fine for what it was, but really wasn't for people of color. When her family was stationed in Europe, they'd occasionally get tickets to hockey games. They'd go. They liked it well enough. But when they got back to the United States, hockey was quickly forgotten. It was football, all the time.

Jackson's assessment is blunt: "How did I perceive hockey? That it's a sport for white people. It was a place for white athletes. And maybe most importantly, it was a sport for white spectators.

"But later, I realized that other people play hockey, they just don't get the airtime."

She admitted that her job gets "even more gigantic" by the day.

"What we accept is that this is going to be a difficult journey, and that we will acknowledge our shortcomings," she said.

What makes it difficult to sell the notion that the culture needs to change is that USA Hockey is not struggling on the ice. In women's hockey, the battle for world supremacy is a simple battle between Canada and the United States. No other nation comes close. One will get gold, one will get silver. The US men's U20 team won the 2023–24 World Junior Championship with relative ease. The new six-team Professional Women's Hockey League has three of its franchises based in the United States. And there are NHL teams that have more American players on their rosters than they do Canadians, something that would have been unthinkable a generation ago. Winning papers over a lot of cracks.

"The traditionalist perspective is very difficult to change, here," said Jackson. "But the stories about marginalized people being treated differently in hockey are far more prevalent than how they thrive and don't feel alone."

Irfan Chaudhry is a teacher and researcher in the field of race, how it relates to the media, and how it affects institutions. He also sits on the Alberta Hate Crimes Committee and Public Safety Canada's Expert Committee on Countering Radicalization to Violence. In 2021, during the height of the pandemic, he received grant money to take a deep dive into race and hockey. As the director of MacEwan University's Office of Human Rights, Diversity, and Equity, he led the Grow the Game summit, a virtual conference that brought together players, media, and scholars on race and hockey. Their sessions were made widely available via YouTube, so you didn't need an invitation to attend.

"I saw a gap," said Chaudhry. "And from the education sector, it was almost a no-brainer. Here was a sector that needed to be exposed to that information."

Speakers talked about microaggressions, racial stereotypes, and the lack of connection hockey fans have to the contributions people of color have made to the game—from the Colored Hockey League that was born in the late nineteenth century in Eastern Canada, to the fact that the most sought-after hockey sticks in the land were once made by the Mi'kmaq people.

In 2023, Hockey Canada hired Chaudhry to become its first-ever vice president of diversity and inclusion. Like Jackson and Davis, Chaudhry is looking at how bias shapes the sport. He believes strongly in looking at demographics and data—and how the power of statistics will overpower stereotypes and unconscious bias. If Hockey Canada knows that there are programs near Black, South Asian, or Indigenous neighborhoods, and the registrars can see the participants are still mainly white, then they know there's a gap in those communities. If Hockey Canada can trace the ages that kids of various backgrounds are more likely to drop out of the sport— or if there are hotspots where players of color all quit at once—then it can be flagged, rather than shrugged off as coincidence. Data is a powerful tool in combating racial stereotypes, and Chaudhry plans to use it.

THE POWER OF SELF-EXAMINATION

In 2022, the NHL issued its first-ever diversity and inclusion report. A new report is scheduled to follow every two years. As of April 2025, we're still waiting for report number two. It reported that the NHL's workforce was nearly 84 percent white. It then recommended that all on-ice officials now undergo diversity and inclusion training, and that all full-time employees in the league's Manhattan headquarters underwent a two-day "Inclusion Learning Experience that explored the dynamics of bias, privilege, and power." The NHL also partnered with Jopwell, a search firm that helps companies diversify their workforces.

The league now has a Player Inclusion Coalition (PIC), which has membership from current and former NHLers, as well as prominent players from the women's game. It advises the NHL on best practices and is headed by retired players—and current broadcasters—P. K. Subban and Anson Carter. In March 2024, members of the PIC finished a tour of all thirty-two dressing rooms in the league. Former players Mark Fraser, Georges Laraque, Jamal Mayers, Al Montoya, and Anthony Stewart led one-hour discussions behind closed dressing room doors about race and diversity. A league statement told the media that the visits emphasized "how inclusion builds the foundation for stronger and higher performing teams."

The PIC also has white members, and Carter has made it clear that inclusion efforts cannot go forward without allyship. In Evan F. Moore and Jashvina Shah's 2021 book, *Game Misconduct: Hockey's Toxic Culture and How to Fix It*, they write about the unfair burden that is often placed on people of color when they're tasked with diversity initiatives without white support.

"In the U.S. and Canada, [diversity] spaces in journalism, education, and the corporate world, among others, are doomed to fail because a white power structure often leaves people of color and women to do the heavy lifting, shouldering the task of fixing the work culture they did not create."[4]

In 2023, Respect Hockey Culture was formed. It's a central service for minor leagues, women's leagues, and junior leagues across North America that provides support on anti-bullying and anti-racism. It's a module that is designed to make players feel comfortable about reporting abuse and racism.

The NHL created a Youth Inclusion Committee, which brought together parents, coaches, and members of Hockey Canada and USA Hockey to discuss the struggles players of color face in grassroots organizations. While the NHL doesn't provide education to the national bodies, it did help provide a platform from which Hockey Canada and USA Hockey could build their own diversity strategies.

"We're trying to do education," said Davis. "Show leadership. Show representation through employment. Market differently. There's not one lever that needs to be pulled; there are multiple cylinders that have to be pulled, simultaneously. And, yes, I think the influence at the youth level is about educating parents and educating coaches."

For the 2023–24 season, the league created a public service announcement that has to be aired in all thirty-two NHL arenas during the games. It warns fans that there is no room for abuse or racism at the rink. There will be no warnings for abusive behavior. Step outside the lines, and it's a game misconduct for the fan.

"Whether you're in Calgary or Detroit, you're getting these same messages that this behavior is not tolerated, and we have zero tolerance for it, and you will get kicked out if you do it," said Davis. "That is major, and that is something that is ultimately going to change the culture of the sport—and it's going to trickle down."

The gloss is definitely on, but is the substance there? Is the NHL living true to Davis's bold vision to diversify the game? It's one thing to talk a good game, it's another to back it up. That's why Davis said repeatedly through our interview that the league has to welcome and embrace "interrogation." It needs to invite the critics in and let them take long, hard looks at the state of the game.

That's what this book will show in the coming chapters. How good has the game been when it comes to following Davis's lead?

"In the sport of hockey, we have embarked on a movement that I would say [in 2018] was not part of the ecosystem of the sport of hockey. It is absolutely part of the ecosystem of hockey, today," said Davis. "Diversity" is a watchword in the NHL's boardrooms. It has become part of NHL Commissioner's Gary Bettman's business gospel.

"We are having conversations today that I can't imagine that the NHL or the sport of hockey, more broadly, could have ever fathomed that we'd be talking about," said Davis. "One of the things I often say around our senior executive table, Gary and I talk about this all the time, is we have to continue to get comfortable with being uncomfortable. Because that is the nexus where you really begin to see change and growth.

"Is it ever going to be perfect? Is it ever going to be that people are thinking that you're doing enough? The answer is no, because the journey of change is a never-ending journey. Whenever you think you've gotten to the destination, the puck moves."

Just a day before I interviewed Davis (in October 2023), what had previously been a private Hockey Quebec report was leaked to the media. It detailed an incident where a teenaged Black player on a Quebec junior team was forced by his white teammates to lie on the ground and utter the words "I can't breathe" while a bully's knee was placed on his neck—mimicking the 2020 murder of George Floyd by Minneapolis police officer Derek Chauvin.

So if the NHL, that "North Star" of the sport, is working hard to shed the image of hockey as a white game, how hard is it to hear that players of color still face brutal hazing rituals—that the rink isn't a welcome place to all?

"You have to stay diligent and committed to this work," said Davis. "It's exhausting, it's hard. It can be very, very discouraging and disappointing when you hear stories like the one from Quebec. But if we really want to see our game improve and to see our sport grow, we have to keep leaning into it. We can't get daunted by the task. We have to continue to do the hard work—and trying not to keep making the same mistakes over and over again.

"When you are trying to impact a huge system, mostly through influence, we don't control every aspect of the hockey ecosystem. And on top of that, the majority of people are interfacing; let's start at the youth level, with kids, our volunteers, that adds another level of complexity onto this."

Hockey has slowly begun a journey that the other three major sports leagues in North America began generations ago. Soccer, as a global game, is its own cultural phenomenon and is hard to compare to the NHL, the National Basketball Association, Major League Baseball, or the North American juggernaut that is the National Football League.

Davis is well aware that many of us believe that hockey is being more proactive only because of the recent scandals that have dogged the game—the revelations that the Chicago Blackhawks covered up the sexual assault of one their own players, Kyle Beach, by Brad Aldrich, a member of their training staff during the team's run to the 2010 Stanley Cup. Hockey Canada has been investigated by a Canadian federal government commission after allegations that five members of the 2018 Canadian national junior team—Carter Hart, Alex Formenton, Michael McLeod, Cal Foote, and Dillon Dube—sexually assaulted a woman in a hotel in London, Ontario. Four of them were playing in the NHL at the time of their arrests in 2024, and Formenton had played for the Ottawa Senators before taking his career to Europe.

The allegations go even further—that Hockey Canada covered up the incident and even have a separate slush fund that, in part, pays off sexual assault victims in exchange for their silence. Major sponsors pulled out, and grassroots hockey organizations threatened to withhold the portions of the registration fees that went to the national organization. The government suspended its financial support of Hockey Canada.

As part of the government inquest, Hockey Canada admitted that it had paid $8.9 million to twenty-one complainants from 1989 to 2022.[5] That's almost one credible sexual assault complainant per year.

And for decades, it went on in silence.

As part of its investigation, the Canadian federal government noted that Hockey Canada's leadership was dominated by white males. How can an organization change when the same old white men who covered up years of abuse are the ones charged with taking the sport in a new direction?

To be fair, the NHL had already hired Davis by the time the news of the allegations broke. But she understands that hockey is continually seen as a sport that's having to react to crises of race, bullying, and assault—and that has to stop.

She said the NHL has to wield its influence on USA Hockey and Hockey Canada—"don't wait until you have a crisis to train your volunteers and your parents."

"The NHL is the North Star of influence, and it could be powerful. Our convening voice could be powerful in connecting from the grassroots youth level all the way up.

"In order for us to have moral authority, we have to lead by example. We have to make sure our own house is in order. So, how do you do both at the same time—continue to improve our own culture, while having credibility and building trust? That is what I refer to as 'earned trust.' It's not granted trust. Earned trust comes from being vulnerable, and showing that you can make mistakes and recover from them. Granted trust is just because of your positionality, people trust you. No, we want earned trust. That means being vulnerable and showing we can recover from the mistakes we make.

"We are imperfect, we will make more mistakes, but we keep trying to do better every single day."

That means the NHL, as the leaders of the sport, has to welcome the hard questions. The league's PR people need to welcome questions that aren't only about what happens on the ice but are also about the social impact of the game.

"I think we are getting more comfortable every day with interrogation," said Davis. "It doesn't mean we're perfect. We're going to make mistakes. That's the thing about change work that's worth understanding—you are not going to be perfect and you are going to make mistakes. I love what Teddy Roosevelt said many, many years ago:

> "It is not the critic who counts; not the man who points out how the strong man stumbles, or where the doer of deeds could have done them better. The credit belongs to the man who is actually in the arena, whose face is marred by dust and sweat and blood; who strives valiantly; who errs, who comes short again and again, because there is no effort without error and shortcoming; but who does actually strive to do the deeds; who knows great enthusiasms, the great devotions…"

"It's the person who leans in and takes the criticism and takes the bumps and bruises."

So how close is the NHL to being the league that Davis envisions it becoming? This is the hard, uncomfortable question that we need to ask—and if we can't get the game aligned to this vision, we may soon be finding NHL games on channel 1322, or on a spotty streaming service that features ads for reverse mortgages, super-absorbent sponges, and kitchen gadgets you never knew you needed.

TWO

WHERE IT'S BEEN

IT'S THE WEEKEND of the 2023 Heritage Classic—highlighted by the big Sunday night tilt that saw the Edmonton Oilers triumph over their fiercest rival, the Calgary Flames, at Commonwealth Stadium in front of 55,411 fans.

By now, outdoor games in the NHL are commonplace. The Heritage Classic. The Stadium Series. The Winter Classic. There's usually three or four of them on the league schedule throughout a given season. Teams wear jerseys that look like they were crafted in the 1930s, celebrity acts play arena rock during the intermissions, and fans struggle to see over the boards from their seats far away in the football stands.

But this Calgary-Edmonton outdoor game was a little different from most; it marked the twentieth anniversary of the Oilers hosting the first modern NHL outdoor game. And with it came plenty of off-the-ice events and celebrations. Alberta's most famous musical export, Nickelback, banged out a cover of Elton John's "Saturday Night's Alright for Fighting" during the second intermission.

The day before the big game, Canada Post hosted a special event in downtown Edmonton's poshest hotel, the JW Marriott. In the hotel's Wayne Gretzky Ballroom, while media and guests noshed on sausage and pastries, the Crown corporation unveiled a new stamp that honored Willie O'Ree, who in 1958 became the first Black player to skate in the NHL.

Banners and posters outside the ballroom carried the black and gold of O'Ree's only NHL club, the Boston Bruins.

Anson Carter, who played for both the Bruins and Oilers during his NHL career, broke from his duties as an analyst for TNT and Sportsnet to emcee the event. Oiler Evander Kane and Flame Nazem Kadri were VIPs at the unveiling. Sarah Nurse, a gold medalist with the Canadian women's team at the 2022 Olympics, was there. And retired fan favorite Georges Laraque and Hall of Fame goaltender Grant Fuhr were spotted sitting close to each other.

Because of his poor health, O'Ree was able to send only a video message of greetings, filmed at his home in San Diego. But the tributes poured in from the VIPs at the event.

"He has become a role model to the entire global community that is connected to this game," said Brian Jennings, the NHL's executive vice president of marketing.

"To be a byproduct of Willie, for me and my family, it gave me a lot of opportunities to succeed in life," said Kane.

"Without Willie O'Ree, there is no Georges Laraque, there is no Anson Carter," said Laraque. "None of us are playing in the NHL. Somebody had to break the barrier in football, baseball, soccer, all those things. But in hockey, you still see today that there are huge obstacles to being a Black guy who wants to play.

"When I was a kid, I was the only Black player playing. He was an adult, the only Black player playing, and he was getting death threats. I never got death threats as a kid. He did. Imagine being alone, and your life is being threatened, just because you're playing a sport. That's another level. If it was hard for me to live through racism, what he went through was inhuman."

O'Ree was feted for his role as the NHL's diversity ambassador, the role he was given in 1998. He became the face of the league's Hockey Is for Everyone program, which celebrates and promotes diversity in the game. According to the league, more than 120,000 boys and girls have participated in Hockey Is for Everyone programs since it was launched.

O'Ree's mantra is famous in the game: "If you think you can, you can. If you think you can't, you're right."

The thing is, a lot of players of color thought they could, but were told they couldn't.

Even though O'Ree emerged as an NHL player in the late 1950s, he had to wait decades for his contributions to the game to be widely recognized. O'Ree's name didn't resonate like Jackie Robinson's did in baseball. In fact, throughout much of the remainder of the twentieth century, he had been relegated to a hockey footnote, a curious bit of trivia for pub nights.

When Laraque made his NHL debut during the 1997–98 season, he knew very little about the first Black man to play in the league. "When I started in the NHL, I knew nothing about Willie O'Ree. When I found out about him, I was mad because I was like, 'how come nobody talks about him?'"

And Laraque was furious to learn that O'Ree was not enshrined in the Hockey Hall of Fame. "I was part of the movement to try and get him inducted into the Hockey Hall of Fame. That was when I started in the NHL, way before all of this. I was a bit frustrated, I was thinking *Why is everyone ignoring this?*"

In his autobiography, O'Ree related that for years and years after he played his final NHL game, he didn't hear from anyone at the league. In 1991, the league invited him to attend the All-Star Game in Chicago— three decades after he played in the league for the final time. It would take another 27 years, and a lot of grassroots campaigns, for O'Ree to finally be inducted into the Hall of Fame as a builder. In 2018, a petition was launched in the New Brunswick capital of Fredericton, O'Ree's hometown. Letters of support came in from across North America—from kids, NHL players, and politicians. Included in those was support from Karl Subban, the father of NHL star and Olympic gold medalist P. K. Subban, NHL goalie Malcolm Subban, and professional player Jordan Subban.[1]

Imagine, if you will, Major League Baseball having to be shamed into recognizing the historical significance of Jackie Robinson. Imagine Robinson's story fading into obscurity. Seems impossible, doesn't it? But that's what happened in the NHL.

O'Ree's name and number hang from the rafters in Boston. After the letter-writing campaign, he made it into the Hall of Fame as a builder. And for a lot of the white establishment in hockey, this is the feel-good stuff that allows us to pat ourselves on the back and congratulate ourselves on how progressive we've become. But when it comes to Black history and how it intersects with hockey, we've barely started the process. Honoring O'Ree does not make up for a plethora of historical wrongs and omissions.

While O'Ree now gets awards named in his honor, the Colored Hockey League, which predated baseball's Negro Leagues by two decades, is still a mystery to most hockey fans. In the Diversity section of the Hockey Hall of Fame, there's a picture with a caption that honors the first professional Black sports league in North America. During Black History Month back in 2021, the Hall's official social media accounts made a single post about the impact of the Colored Hockey League. But that's about it. There are no players or builders from the Colored Hockey League who have been enshrined in the Hall of Fame, though the league is credited with many hockey innovations that changed the game, including the slap shot.

Major League Baseball preserves Negro Leagues stats. You can buy a Homestead Grays cap at any Lids or Fanatics outlet. The Pittsburgh Pirates even wore Homestead Grays jerseys for a theme night. As of the writing of this book, there were thirty-seven players of color who have been enshrined in the National Baseball Hall of Fame for their contributions in the Negro Leagues, beginning with Satchel Paige's induction in 1971.[2]

I'd be willing to bet quite a bit of money that most of my colleagues in the press box would be hard pressed to name a Colored Hockey League team, let alone a player from that era. To be fair, before the 2020s, I would have been one of those media members who would have met that question with a blank stare and a sheepish shrug.

There is still very little out there to make us all more aware of these groundbreakers and pioneers. And it's fair to say there really is nothing out there that's considered mainstream hockey viewing and reading. The league is covered in filmmaker Damon Kwame Mason's 2015 release, *Soul on Ice: Past, Present & Future*, and it informs *Black Ice*, a documentary from Hubert Davis that was released in 2022. And there is George and Darril Fosty's excellent work in documenting the history of the Colored Hockey League.

As the Fostys wrote:

"Twenty-five years before the Negro Baseball Leagues in the United States, and twenty-two years before the birth of the National Hockey League, Black Canadians helped pioneer the sport of ice hockey, changing this winter game from the primitive 'gentleman's past-time' of the nineteenth century to the modern fast-moving game of today. Led by skilled and educated leadership, the Colored Hockey League would emerge as a premier force in Canadian hockey and supply the resilience necessary to preserve a unique culture; a culture that exists to this day. Unfortunately, such was their fate, that their contributions were conveniently ignored, or simply stolen, as White teams and hockey officials, influence by the Black league, copied elements of Black style or sought to take self-credit for Black hockey innovations."[3]

Throughout the writing of this book, I'd heard players of color tell me how important representation is in the game. They told me over and over that hockey is traditionally a "white man's game." How could the narrative be changed if the history of the Colored Hockey League was as widely known as the Montreal Canadiens dynasties of the 1950s and the 1970s, or the Edmonton Oilers dynasty of the 1980s? How would perceptions be changed if Eddie Martin's slap shot was as iconic an image as Bobby Orr leaping through the air as he cemented a Stanley Cup win for the Boston Bruins?

Hall of Fame forward Jarome Iginla wrote the foreword for O'Ree's autobiography. Right there, on page one, he recalls a novice tournament held just outside Edmonton, where he was told "Black people don't play hockey."[4]

I am writing this chapter while sitting at a sports pub in St. Albert, the Edmonton suburb where Iginla first fell in love with the game. And I think about how the "white man's game" narrative is recycled, generation through generation. Would Iginla have grown up hearing that Black-people-don't-play-hockey trope if parents, coaches, and administrators knew that the history of the game wasn't nearly as white as they thought? It is our collective shame that we've allowed the Colored Hockey League to be the bailiwick of just a select few historians.

Maybe the reason we're not comfortable with the topic of the Colored Hockey League is that it forces a lot of us to ask uncomfortable questions about the historical relationship between Canada and the United States. After all, our countries are supposed to be fast friends, no? While there are a few far-right politicians in the United States who go on about the world's longest unprotected border, and Canadians will smugly roll their eyes about America's private health care system, the truth is that our border is basically invisible.

But the origins of the Colored Hockey League come from a time when the relationship between the countries was very different.

Many of the league's players could trace their family histories back to Black men who chose to wear redcoats. These men were promised freedom and land if they fought with the British against the American Revolutionaries. Or players could trace their roots to men who fought for the British in the War of 1812. While slavery wouldn't be abolished in the British colonies until 1834, it was limited in Upper Canada in 1793. Similar promises were made; land and freedom—all you had to do was survive the war. After the ends of both of those conflicts, the British refused to return American "property" after the cessations of hostilities. (As in, enslaved people.) The land the Black soldiers received in exchange for their services was by no means prime real estate. The men who took the offer were not naive. They knew that they were signing a blood bargain; the Brits weren't giving up a heck of a lot, and the risks were deadly. But given the choice of living in a slave state or being at the bottom of the social ladder in the loyalist colonies, it was an easy decision to make for many Black men.

The establishment of Black communities such as Africville, located just outside Halifax, is not something that's easily taught in American schools because it casts the years of conflict between the Americans and British as not so clear-cut when it comes to right and wrong.

And there's another layer of historical complexity to add to this all. The Eastern Canadian communities that hosted Colored Hockey League teams had been the end points on the Underground Railroad, which led to a promised land for escaped enslaved people.

The Colored Hockey League was rooted in its anti-Americanism. (Try selling that on a Black History theme night in an American NHL arena.) The team names honored the Underground Railroad. The Moss Backs got their name from the fact that escaping enslaved people, running through forests at night, knew that moss only grew on the north sides of trees. It's the moss that helped the escapees keep their bearings as they headed north toward Canada. The Dartmouth Jubilees celebrated not a royal anniversary but a word that freedom seekers and their children used to describe the passage of Britain's emancipation edicts.

The Fostys wrote of a league that began as a way for Black churches to attract more followers, especially during the winter months. It evolved into a cultural movement: "The Colored Hockey League was more than just a sports organization; it was, in fact, the first Black Pride sports movement in history—truly a magnificent undertaking, considering nothing like it had ever been attempted, either before or since."[5]

But there was one team name that stood out above the others. Africville was a Black settlement that was close to Halifax, and its team was called the Sea-Sides. The jersey featured a double-S logo. But it meant a lot more to freedom seekers and their descendants; the double-S insignia was modeled after the brand that slave owners used to permanently scar the faces of captured "slave stealers."

"In terms of historic significance, the Sea-Sides uniform is perhaps the most important hockey uniform ever made," wrote the Fosty brothers.[6] But no replica of that uniform hangs in the Hall of Fame.

How can something that vital, so important to Canadian, American, and hockey history, simply be *lost*? Maybe it's because recognizing teams like the Africville Sea-Sides would be a bridge too far in arenas where unquestioned patriotism is part of the price of admission. We like our history to be cut and dried, with clear heroes and villains.

The story of Black hockey is complicated because, even in Commonwealth-lovin' Canada, which is so heavily influenced by American media, we simplify the Revolution to a battle between the "bad guys," the British monarchists, against the "good guys," the American patriots of the thirteen rebel colonies. Nuance doesn't exist when Mel Gibson plays *The Patriot* on screen or Lin-Manuel Miranda takes the stage in order to take "My Shot" in *Hamilton*. It's uncomfortable to recognize the historical truth that many people of color in the thirteen colonies fled to the British side because the freedom offered by the Crown was a lot better than being treated as property by the American "freedom" fighters. The names of the teams in the Colored Hockey League, and the bloodlines of the players who participated in it, are reminders of just how many people fled the colonies for what the Brits called "The Promised Land" of Eastern Canada. To remember the Colored Hockey League would shift the American Revolution into a different historical perspective than the one offered by what kids are taught in history class, where the Founding Fathers are seen with almost religious fervor.

There is also shame on the north side of the border. Many of the players, and the children of these players, had their "Promised Land" snatched away by white rail barons and city governments, who took their settlements to build steel ties and harbors. Canada, the supposed sanctuary for those who traveled the Underground Railroad, would show that segregation, division, and intimidation of Blacks was not limited to the south side of the border.

Unlike baseball's Negro Leagues, the Colored Hockey League barely qualifies as a footnote in the Hockey Hall of Fame. No players who stood out in this league have their plaques hung in the famed Great Hall in downtown Toronto. No NHL team has worn a Colored Hockey League jersey, like the Pirates did with the Homestead Grays. It may have taken decades for Willie O'Ree to get his due, but there remains a gaping void when it comes to setting the historical record straight about Black contributions to the game, when the sport was still in its infancy.

The Colored Hockey League began in 1895, when the game was still played seven a side, with two halves rather than three periods, and before standardized hockey nets were introduced. It would survive the First World War and the Halifax Explosion of 1917, and it would be the seeding ground for barnstorming American Black teams of the 1920s and 1930s, such as the Colored Panthers and the Colored Monarchs.

It could be argued that the Colored Hockey League gave us hockey's first free-agent controversy, when star player Eddie "Stonewall" Martin left the powerhouse Halifax Eurekas to play for the Africville Sea-Sides. Martin may indeed have been the man to invent the slap shot. The Eurekas' indignation was so great over losing Martin, the team refused to play the Sea-Sides if the player dressed. Martin would be the easy pick for enshrinement into hockey's hallowed hall.

Should there be a mention in the Hall of Fame of Henry "Braces" Franklyn, who reportedly was less than four feet tall but was a star goalie in the early days of the league because of his simple innovation, to flop to the ice when needed?

Or what of the founders of the league, who used hockey as a beacon to point out the systemic racism that was commonplace in Eastern Canada, even though Blacks had been promised land and opportunity in exchange for their loyalty to the Crown? Should James A. R. Kinney, James Robinson Johnston, and Henry Sylvester Williams not be considered hallowed "builders" of the game—and be at least considered for the Hall on those grounds?

Avry Lewis-McDougall is a Black Canadian hockey journalist who has called for the Hall of Fame to change its induction process. Year after year, the classes are dominated by white NHL alumni. Yes, women are now regularly part of the classes, but they can never outnumber the men in a given year. And contributions from other leagues are ignored.

Lewis-McDougall has written that the Hall's refusal to recognize John Paris Jr., who in 1994 became the first Black head coach to win a minor pro championship when he led the Atlanta Knights to the International Hockey League title, needs to be rectified.

"Transparency in voting is also another matter that needs to be a reality," Lewis-McDougall wrote of the Hall.[7] "In basketball, baseball, and football, there's a level of openness regarding the voters and voting numbers at various levels in those other three sports. When it comes to hockey, we know that the Hall of Fame selection committee votes on who gets in, with 75 percent being the barrier to entry for induction; with that being said, we don't know who votes for who or who doesn't get enough votes."

The nature of this book—taking a hard look at race and hockey—will make it seem like there are more villains than heroes in the hockey world. But we should celebrate the likes of Martin and Franklyn as heroic figures. As famed American philosopher Susan Neiman writes, heroes give even the worst of societies someone to admire, ideals that can be held up to the light.

"Heroes close the gap between what ought to be and what is," Neiman wrote in her 2023 book *Left Is Not Woke*. "They show that it's not only possible to use our freedom to stand against injustice, but that some people actually did so."[8]

Neiman was writing about white civil rights activists in the Deep South, activists who a lot of us, stereotypically, refuse to believe existed. So her words can be applied to hockey-playing Black activists, who came by their activism not by choice but as a way of life.

The thing is, O'Ree did know about the Colored Hockey League. Growing up in Eastern Canada in the 1940s and early 1950s, O'Ree was just a generation removed from that history. It fueled his dream to be an NHLer. Sure, there was yet to be a Black player in the NHL, but he didn't grow up with the falsehood that "Black people don't play hockey."

"I knew then that I could play hockey with the big guys," O'Ree wrote in his autobiography.[9] "I also knew that there hadn't yet been a Black man who played pro in the NHL, even though Black humans had been playing hockey for as long as white humans had."

O'Ree's ancestry, like many of the players in the Colored Hockey League, can be traced back to escaped enslaved people. According to O'Ree, his great-great-granddad escaped the United States in the late eighteenth century. Paris O'Ree's South Carolina slavery began when he was granted to a former American Revolutionary officer as a reward for service.

O'Ree's story is inspirational. He had to cover up the fact he could see out of only one eye—because it would have prevented him from playing in the NHL. His spot in the Hockey Hall of Fame, though belated, is well deserved.

WILLIE WAS FIRST, WHO WAS SECOND?

On April 15 of every season, every Major League Baseball player ditches his regular jersey and replaces it with one with number 42 on the back. The name bars are gone. No player gets his name on the back of his jersey on that day.

That's because 42 stands on its own. It's a number synonymous with one of the greatest legends in baseball history—and one of the most important agents for social change in North America.

On that day in 1947, Jackie Robinson made his Brooklyn Dodgers' debut, becoming the first Black man to play in a Major League Baseball game. And this signing would soon bring an end to baseball's segregated system, separating the Negro Leagues from the Majors.

Now, it would be trivial of me to state that change wasn't difficult, or that racism in baseball was miraculously eradicated over the course of one game or even one season. It was not an easy thing for Robinson to take this on his shoulders. He was thrown at by pitchers, in an era before batting helmets. He heard the slurs from the stands and opposing dugouts. But one thing that couldn't be denied was his talent. He was named the National League rookie of the year in '47, and, through his decorated, World Series–winning career, would be named an All-Star six times. As Hall of Famers go, he was about as automatic a choice as they come and not just because of the color of his skin. He had Hall of Fame skills as a player.

But maybe even more important than what he did on the diamond, his appearance opened the doors for Black players across America. In 1971, the soon-to-be-World Series champion Pittsburgh Pirates made history when the team fielded a lineup made up entirely of Black and Latino players.

Compare that with the NHL. For a baseball fan, it's easy to rattle off the names of legendary players of color after Robinson's breakthrough in 1947. Willie Mays. Hank Aaron. Roberto Clemente. Bob Gibson. But die-hard hockey fans who know that Willie O'Ree was the league's first Black player would be hard pressed to name the second. (Cheers to you if you know it was former Washington Capital Mike Marson.)

The NHL has named their diversity award after Willie O'Ree. You will lose count of the times the NHL and the hockey establishment call Willie O'Ree the Jackie Robinson of hockey. But let's be clear, there is a bit of revisionist history going on.

O'Ree became the first Black player to appear in the league—for the Boston Bruins—in the 1957–58 season. Before that, there were many BIPOC players who excelled in the amateur and minor pro ranks but could not make it to the NHL because of the color of their skin. The NHL didn't want Black players, Asian players, or Indigenous players. That was also true of Major League Baseball. While Robinson was a mercurial talent, there were many other worthy players of color who came before him—but the doors to Major League stadiums were closed to them, unless they bought tickets to watch games from their spots in segregated stands.

Unlike Robinson, O'Ree did not have a storied career. Yet, during his brief time as a pro, he faced many of the same abuses on the ice that Robinson faced on the baseball diamond: opposing players trying to deliberately injure him, and fans hurling racial abuse and objects when he stepped on the ice. O'Ree suspected that the Bruins traded him in 1961 because they had discovered that he was blind in one eye. Despite excelling in minor pro hockey, from Quebec to California, O'Ree never returned to the NHL.

He was attacked by fans while sitting in the penalty box in Chicoutimi, Quebec. And there was a stick-swinging battle with Chicago Black Hawks star Eric Nesterenko, who peppered O'Ree with N-word insults before the Bruins' winger snapped.

"It was deliberate," O'Ree said. "We didn't wear helmets then. I hit him over the head with my stick, and we got into a fight. Both benches emptied. I had to remain with the doctor the entire game with two police officers standing outside the door."[10]

And when O'Ree took over the NHL's diversity initiatives, he'd get death threats in the mail, like this: "We know there are players of your kind in Canada, but you don't need to bring them to the States."[11]

The racial basis of the incident was never reported; the "color blind" media saw it as a good, old-fashioned battle. O'Ree never even told his parents why it happened.

Jackie Robinson played ten full seasons in Major League ball, leading the Dodgers to a World Series win in 1955. Willie O'Ree only played a total of forty-five NHL games, about half a season's worth of appearances. He played just two games in 1957–58, the season he broke the NHL color barrier and then was sent back down to the minors to wait three years before the Bruins called him up again.

This is in no way meant to disparage O'Ree's accomplishments. In 2022, fittingly, the Bruins retired his No. 22 jersey.

"I will never forget how my teammates in the Bruins locker room accepted me as one of their own," O'Ree said during his jersey retirement ceremony. "This was a time when some of the fans and opposing players were not ready to see a Black man in the NHL. When I became the first, I remembered the advice my older brother, Richard, gave me…he was not only my brother and my friend but my mentor. He used to say 'Willie, focus on your goals you set for yourself, work hard and stay positive.' This is what I tried to do as a member of the Bruins every time I put on the jersey."

But when the NHL and the hockey establishment equate his career to Robinson's, it inflates the league's story of inclusion and diversity. It would take thirteen years before Marson skated in the NHL. Think about it. The

Pirates fielded an all-BIPOC lineup three years *before* the NHL's second Black player made his debut.

Marson would play 196 games in the NHL, more than four times the number of games skated in by O'Ree. There were racial slurs on and off the ice, death threats from opposing fans, and microaggressions as security personnel in other arenas and hotels would refuse him entry not believing a Black man could play in the NHL.

He recalled his early days in the league in an interview that appeared on the Washington Capitals official website.[12] "It wasn't just that I was a 19-year-old kid playing professional hockey," Marson said. "I was the only kid in the world who was Black and playing at that time. And with all of the different social ramifications and setups that were going on at that time in America, it was completely unheard of.

"It was a daily issue of things that were almost mind blowing. There were times when I was refused lodging in hotels and the team would have to stick up for me. Or entering an arena like say, Madison Square Garden, and being questioned by security staff because there were no Black hockey players. So, to their credit, they were asking the right questions, only to find out that yes, I was playing for Washington. For me, this was a daily thing. You'd go to pre-board an airplane and you're questioned—'Well sir, I'm sorry this is just for the hockey players.' I dealt with this kind of business all the time."

In the same story, former teammate Ron Lalonde noted that all the abuse Marson had to deal with impacted his game. "[The racism] was overt on the ice, and he played an aggressive style," said Lalonde, who played with Marson for parts of four seasons. "He played like he had a chip on his shoulder. That's how he played in junior—rough and tough. But guys in the NHL started to challenge him and you'd hear things that would get anybody upset and riled. Unfortunately, he had to spend too much time fighting and trying to defend himself rather than working on his game. He had the physical skills, but he needed some coaching and some patience and fitting in. You'd hear things from some of the tougher players in the league because they knew they could get him off of his game pretty quick.

"There were racial slurs that were fired, and he'd be quick [to react]. He had a short fuse. The next thing you knew, he'd be involved in something. It was hard for him to work on his game. And he could skate. He was one of the best skaters in the league, but he spent so much energy having to defend himself."

Val James was the first Black American-born player to make it to the NHL. He made his Buffalo Sabres debut during the 1981–82 season, more than two decades after O'Ree made his NHL bow. In James's autobiography, *Black Ice*, there's something on the back cover that jumps out. It's a blurb from ESPN's John Saunders. "My brother, Bernie, was the fifth Black player to reach the NHL, and we both know the challenges that come with being the lone face in not only the locker room, but the league."[13]

Players of color have come into the NHL at such a glacial pace that it's easy to list them in order of their appearances. *One*. Years pass. *Two*. More years pass. *Three*. And so on.

It's also dangerous for us to slap ourselves on the back and talk about O'Ree or even Robinson "breaking" color barriers. Robinson got to the Major League because Branch Rickey, a white president in what was an all-white league, said so. O'Ree got his chance where others like Herb Carnegie and Larry Kwong did not because the white management of the Bruins opened the door to their dressing room.

In her book *White Fragility*, Robin DiAngelo asks her readers to reframe how history has portrayed the story of Jackie Robinson making the move to the Major Leagues. In movies like *42*, or how the Major Leagues celebrated Jackie Robinson Day once a year, you might be fooled into thinking that Robinson *broke* the barrier that had prevented Blacks from playing. Instead, DiAngelo notes that there were many great Black players who existed before Robinson; the difference was that the Dodgers organization allowed Robinson through the door. She wrote that we should call Jackie Robinson "the first Black man whites allowed to make Major League Baseball."[14]

Likewise, O'Ree, while being no doubt a pioneer, had the door opened for him by the white ownership of the Boston Bruins. He was by no means the first player of color to excel in the amateur or junior ranks.

THOSE WHO CAME BEFORE WILLIE

Herb Carnegie was arguably the best player to never play in the NHL.

Throughout the 1940s and 1950s, Carnegie was an offensive force in the Quebec senior men's leagues—at the time, it offered some of the best levels of competition outside the NHL. One season, he scored 127 points in just 56 games for Sherbrooke. But as a Black man, Carnegie's glass ceiling was the minor pros.

The words in Carnegie's autobiography, *A Fly in a Pail of Milk*, drip with anger. Carnegie played with elite junior teams in Toronto and rubbed shoulders with many future NHLers. As the story goes, famed Maple Leafs owner Conn Smythe, whose name remains on the trophy that goes to the MVP of the NHL playoffs, was famous for wanting his hockey team to be the most Canadian stereotype of "loyal" that it could be—white and Protestant. He saw Carnegie play, and the following quote was relayed to the player, that Smythe "would give $10,000 to the person who could turn Carnegie white."

Famed hockey ref and broadcaster Red Storey vouched that it was true.

"My mind was a maelstrom," wrote Carnegie. "I can't remember exactly what I thought, but a little voice in the back of my head was kissing my NHL hopes goodbye…My dream was dashed, shattered. It's a horrible feeling to realize that opportunity has been unfairly snatched from your hand by such dastardly means."[15]

Carnegie was a teammate of future Montreal Canadiens great Jean Béliveau with the Quebec Aces. Béliveau wrote the foreword in Carnegie's autobiography.

Carnegie excelled in the minor pros. He; his brother, Ossie; and Manny McIntyre joined together to become the first all-Black line outside of the history of the Colored Hockey League. Throughout the 1940s, they played together in towns far removed from the NHL: Timmins, Ontario; Shawinigan, Quebec; and Sherbrooke, Quebec.

When the Second World War erupted, Carnegie was rejected for military service. He was the wrong color for the NHL, and he was the wrong color to wear Canadian military greens. NHL rosters thinned as players went to military camps—precious few actually saw action. Carnegie hoped to get his chance. But it never came, even though Carnegie failed his military exam. In a league that was down to just six teams, he knew that if the most influential owner in the league was so adamant about keeping players of color out of the league, the others would hold the party line.

Finally, at nearly thirty years of age, Carnegie was invited to the New York Rangers' training camp in 1948. He was offered the chance to go to the minors. He thought that race was the reason he wasn't given a clear path to the NHL team. He turned down multiple offers to play in the Broadway Blueshirts' minor-league system. He knew he was at an age where he couldn't afford to languish as an elder statesman playing with up-and-coming prospects.

Even when a car accident forced the Rangers to remove two starting forwards from their roster, Carnegie was never asked to come back. While there are those who might say that Carnegie exiled himself, the fact is, he never got a second chance (there'll be more about the lack of second chances for hockey players of color in a later chapter).

Carnegie's daughter, Bernice, is an author and public speaker, and talks about how much still needs to be done in the game of hockey—today and beyond. "It's not just hockey," she said. "We're behind everywhere when it comes to diversity. This is a battle that—for people of color, anyway—[we've been] dealing with since we were brought over in boats. It's an ongoing issue. It's always going to be there. It's up to those of us who believe that we can do better, that we can interact in a respectful and kinder way, to keep pushing that narrative.

"We know this is ongoing, but we need to at least take a positive approach to making those changes. If we don't have positive voices that can keep speaking to these issues, where are we? We're not going to get ahead at all. We have to have people speaking up. We have to have people listening with open ears, not just glancing over things and doing something for the moment. This is a long-term vision for what humanity is about."

When I spoke with Bernice, she told me that her dad would exchange letters with another player whose NHL hopes were curtailed by racism— Larry Kwong.

Kwong broke the NHL's color barrier on March 13, 1948, suiting up for the same Rangers team that had offered Carnegie a tryout. So, you might wonder, why isn't he more celebrated by the league? Why is his name so unfamiliar to hockey fans?

That's because his NHL career lasted exactly one shift.

Kwong was a Chinese Canadian hockey phenom from Vernon, British Columbia. In the professional minor leagues, during the mid-1940s, he was averaging over a point per game. At that time, with only six NHL teams in existence, the minors were filled with players who were damn good.

NHL teams controlled contracts to the point that it was impossible for a minor leaguer to move unless the big-league team that owned his rights gave the say-so. An example: in the early 1950s, the Edmonton Flyers, the farm team of the Detroit Red Wings, was stacked. The Red Wings were winning Stanley Cup after Stanley Cup, so it was nearly impossible for a guy excelling in the minors to break into the parent club. The result was a Flyers team that was a juggernaut in the minor pros, led by future Hall of Fame goaltender Glenn Hall.

Hall said that the Flyers were so good, they would have given the Chicago Black Hawks, one of the worst teams in the NHL at the time, a run for their money. Surely, the Flyers weren't as good as the Red Wings or the Montreal Canadiens, but the Flyers could have competed with the bottom tier of the parent league.

"They probably would have beat us, but we would have made them sweat to do it," Hall told me back in 2005.[16]

So, for Kwong to finally get the call to leave minor-league purgatory and get the chance to play for the Rangers, it was a big deal. Or, at least, it seemed like a big deal. He didn't hit the ice until the third period. He was on the ice, and then he was off. That was it. An entire NHL career, gone in seconds.

A Calgary-based group called Hockey 4 Youth has launched a campaign called #ItsLarrysTurn to have Kwong enshrined in the Hockey Hall of Fame (he is in the BC Sports Hall of Fame). As of early 2023, it had over nine thousand signees.

Kwong's fans aren't the only ones pushing for recognition for a player of color whose exploits are in danger of being forgotten. Consider the story of Kenneth Moore, from the Peepeekisis First Nation in Saskatchewan. He emerged as a hockey phenom in the late 1920s. In 1930, he scored a late third-period goal to give his Regina Pats the Memorial Cup.

The Memorial Cup goes to the top junior hockey team in Canada, and many of Moore's Regina Pats' teammates would go on to play in the NHL. Gordon Pettinger, who was on the ice when Moore scored the Cup-clinching goal, would go on to a long NHL career and won Stanley Cups as a member of the Rangers, Detroit Red Wings, and Boston Bruins. While Pettinger leapfrogged from Regina into the pro ranks, Moore had to remain an amateur, but he played for Canada at the 1932 Winter

Olympics. Canada won—and Moore became the first Indigenous Canadian to be an Olympic gold medalist.

But the NHL was never an option for Moore. He would win two Allan Cups, which go to the best senior amateur team in Canada. At that time, with the NHL having ten teams, prior to the attrition that would lead to the postwar "Original Six," there weren't a lot of jobs at the top levels of hockey. Many of the senior amateur teams were darn good and would be followed feverishly by their fan bases.

Even though he passed away in 1981, Moore's family continues to push for him to be inducted into Canada's Sports Hall of Fame.[17]

So how do we lift the veil and honor those who have been forgotten? Queen's University sociologist Courtney Szto is the coauthor of the *Policy Paper for Anti-Racism in Canadian Hockey*, which was presented to members of Hockey Canada and the NHL in 2019. She said that kids need to learn about the multicolored history of the game when they first get onto the ice. If we can teach them how to skate, we can teach them about the contributions made to the game by Asian, Black, and Indigenous innovators.

"The ability to avoid learning about racism is a privilege," Szto said during the virtual Grow the Game summit.[18] "If hockey is Canada's game, every Canadian child should know about the Colored Hockey League of the Maritimes, and how Mi'kmaq carvers made the best hockey sticks of the turn of the century. The game has always belonged to all of us, just not in equal measure or recognition."

In 2021, the Greater Toronto Hockey League welcomed a new organization into the fold. Seaside Hockey had seventy-six players registered in its inaugural season, and the numbers nearly doubled in year two.[19] The team's mission statement is to provide "assistance to visible minority youths in the GTA community to play hockey by removing financial barriers." But the name is telling—someone is finally honoring the history of the Colored Hockey League. Someone is teaching kids that hockey's history isn't exclusively white. The ghosts of Africville are finally being heard. It's a start.

Szto and her colleagues, Sam McKegney, Mike Auksi, and Bob Dawson, presented their policy paper in 2019 at Queen's University. The NHL, which is supposed to be the "North Star" of hockey culture, according to Kim Davis, sent representatives to the presentation. But there wasn't representation from major junior hockey leagues and, most telling, the local minor-hockey organizations in Kingston, Ontario. Szto later spoke at the Grow the Game online hockey summit organized by Irfan Chaudhry, as discussed in chapter 1. So, in a roundabout way, we can hope this work is now getting the due it deserved when it was first released.

"The reason we need to have higher expectations for hockey with respect to anti-racism in Canada is because of its history as part of the larger colonial project," said Szto. That's because hockey played a role in residential schools—one of the most egregious examples of institutional racism as you'll find in North American history. For the non-Canadian readers—our nation isn't quite what you might think it is; we're not all polite and rather harmless. From the nineteenth century until the final federally run residential school closed in the 1990s, the Canadian and provincial governments, along with the Roman Catholic Church, established a system that was designed to whitewash the country's Indigenous people.

Duncan Campbell Scott, a Canadian writer and politician who helped expand residential schools in the early part of the twentieth century, said this: "Our object is to continue until there is not a single Indian in Canada that has not been absorbed into the body politic."[20]

Children were taken away from their Indigenous families. They were whisked out of their communities to faraway residential schools. There are many historical accounts of neglect, beatings, and sexual assault. Kids were taught that their Indigenous cultures were worthless; their languages and, oftentimes, their given names, were erased. Only now is Canada as a whole coming to grips with the fact that scores of children died in these schools. In 2021, researchers, using ground-penetrating radar, found 215 anomalies, which may indicate the remains of children at the site of a former residential school in Kamloops, British Columbia.

It is a national shame.

In 2022, Pope Francis apologized for the Catholic Church's role in residential schools.

But what does it have to do with hockey? The schools used hockey as a lure—that Indigenous families who sent their children away could expect that at least their sons would be given colorful hockey sweaters and shiny new equipment. They were told that the boys would be placed in school leagues. Hockey was part of the big lie that was being sold, and this is something we shouldn't forget.

Fred Sasakamoose, the first Treaty Indigenous player to skate in the NHL, wrote in his autobiography that hockey was his only respite during his stay at the St. Michael's residential school near Duck Lake, Saskatchewan. He was sexually assaulted by other boys, had hot oil poured on his head as punishment, and even dug graves for other children.

"From time to time, a few boys would be brought out there, given shovels, and told to dig," Sasakamoose wrote in his autobiography, *Call Me Indian*.[21] "We weren't there when the long, deep holes were filled. And no signs or plaques marked the freshly mounded earth."

And he recalled that when his school hockey team hosted white clubs from nearby Saskatchewan towns, the priests put on a gloss the students never saw on a regular day. After the game, the two teams would be treated to a fine postgame meal, including fine cuts of meat and even dessert. The ritual of hosting a hockey game at a residential school was even more about the public relations exercise than it was about sport.

It was sportswashing, years before that term became part of our vernacular. Sports has always been used to gloss over the barbarities of oppressive regimes—from the Soviets and their Olympic program, to the Chilean soccer team that played in the 1974 World Cup, with players forced to go to West Germany under threat of punishment from General Pinochet. The world was pretty much OK with having a World Cup played in Qatar, with stadiums built by indentured foreign workers—thousands of whom disappeared during the construction of these sporting palaces. We see it now with Saudi Arabia's takeover of professional golf, or that country's hosting of a glamorous Formula 1 race. While we like to think of sports as a great equalizer, it's often placed in the shop window as a distraction—and we place more importance on the shiny lights than what lies underneath.

Sasakamoose played just eleven NHL games. After spending a year and part of a second in the minors, he decided to return home to his reserve in Saskatchewan. It's clear from reading his memoir that the trauma of residential schools deeply affected him as a hockey player. Being moved around by the Black Hawks organization, being dispatched back and forth from the pros to the minors, made him feel like nothing more than a name and a number. Just as he did at residential school, he felt like he was property, not a person.

When he returned home, he faced constant questions: Why did he give up on the NHL dream?

"I couldn't explain how hard it had been to live in that world. To always hide some important part of you, to keep so much of your past a secret from the only people you could call friends. To wonder if people thought differently about you because you were an Indian. To have no one to talk to who might have understood how it felt when someone made a hurtful or insensitive comment. To be powerless in a system that made you feel like a checker piece being moved around on a huge, unfamiliar board."[22]

After hearing from residential school survivors, Canada's Truth and Reconciliation Commission released 94 Calls to Action. Five of them dealt with sport.

87. We call upon all levels of government, in collaboration with Aboriginal peoples, sports halls of fame, and other relevant organizations, to provide public education that tells the national story of Aboriginal athletes in history.

88. We call upon all levels of government to take action to ensure long-term Aboriginal athlete development and growth, and continued support for the North American Indigenous Games, including funding to host the games and for provincial and territorial team preparation and travel.

89. We call upon the federal government to amend the Physical Activity and Sport Act to support reconciliation by ensuring that policies to promote physical activity as a fundamental element of health and well-being, reduce barriers to sports participation, increase the pursuit of excellence in sport, and build capacity in the Canadian sport system, are inclusive of Aboriginal peoples.

90. We call upon the federal government to ensure that national sports policies, programs, and initiatives are inclusive of Aboriginal peoples, including, but not limited to, establishing:

i. In collaboration with provincial and territorial governments, stable funding for, and access to, community sports programs that reflect the diverse cultures and traditional sporting activities of Aboriginal peoples.

ii. An elite athlete development program for Aboriginal athletes.

iii. Programs for coaches, trainers, and sports officials that are culturally relevant for Aboriginal peoples.

iv. Anti-racism awareness and training programs.

91. We call upon the officials and host countries of international sporting events such as the Olympics, Pan Am, and Commonwealth games to ensure that Indigenous peoples' territorial protocols are respected, and local Indigenous communities are engaged in all aspects of planning and participating in such events.[23]

While all are important, Call to Action 87 ties into Szto's call for us all to better understand that hockey history isn't solely the domain of white males. While it's important for minor-hockey coaches to understand their Xs and Os, they should also be required to at least have a working understanding of where the game has been, so they can better see where it needs to go.

THREE

WHERE WE ARE

U SUALLY, THE MONTH of August is when you find NHLers at their summer homes, enjoying the final weeks of the off-season break. If you ever want to find a big-league player in the middle of the summer, just try your luck and knock on a random cabin door in British Columbia's Shuswap—it's like the Riviera for hockey players.

But 2020 was a hell of a year. The COVID-19 pandemic forced the NHL to pause its season in March, with about a month's worth of games left to go. In the summer, the decision was made to finish the season by holding the playoffs in what were essentially arenas transformed into soundstages. Half the playoff teams quarantined in Edmonton, while the other half headed to Toronto. They played in bubble environments, with high-security measures. No fans were allowed.

But as sports leagues got back to work, all of North America was following the news coming from the Twin Cities of Minneapolis and St. Paul. We all watched George Floyd being murdered by police officers over and over. Outrage and protests followed around the world. The Black Lives Matter movement grew.

As the NHL staged its playoffs in empty arenas, the newly formed Hockey Diversity Alliance, founded by a group of NHL BIPOC players, found its voice. Matt Dumba, then a defenseman for the Minnesota Wild, was selected to make an impassioned plea for racism in hockey to end, which would be broadcast on national television, ahead of Game 1 of a playoff series between the Edmonton Oilers and Chicago Blackhawks.

With no fans in attendance, and just the Hawks and Oilers players standing on their respective blue lines, Dumba walked out into the spotlight. There was no crowd, no buzz in the arena; it was made all the clearer that Dumba was making a made-for-TV appearance.

"We vow to stand up for justice and fight for what is right," Dumba said, voice cracking. "I know, firsthand, as a minority playing the great game of hockey, the unexplainable and difficult challenges that come with it. The Hockey Diversity Alliance and the NHL want kids to feel safe, comfortable, and free-minded every time they enter an arena. So, I stand in front of you today on behalf of those groups and promise that we will fight against injustice. We will fight for what is right. I hope this inspires a new generation of hockey players and hockey fans.

"Hockey is a great game, but it could be a whole lot greater—and it starts with all of us."

Dumba plays in front of thousands of people a night in NHL arenas. But that night, in an empty Rogers Place, the Edmonton Oilers' home arena, he trembled like never before.

"I was as nervous as hell," he recalled in a lengthy interview he did for this book. "I knew that so many people would be watching, and I heard my voice echo back, it went through me, because we were in an empty arena. It was a crazy experience, but I was glad I was able to make it through and get what I needed to say out there."

What the millions of people watching on television didn't know was that before Dumba went to center ice to make the address, there was talk about aborting the whole thing. Dumba said he knew that his anti-racism message didn't have the support of the entire NHL community.

"I know for a fact that when I was giving my speech, there were several teams that reached out to the NHL and said to get this off their TV, that they were going to lose their fan base," said Dumba. "There were teams that pushed back that they wouldn't stand for it. They were more concerned about fans with fucking hate in their heart than they were people of color who are involved in the game."

This is one of the contradictions that surround the NHL and hockey as a whole. A lot is said about making the game more diverse, but it's hard to pull the old guard along. The culture is strong, and it is resilient. Dumba's allegations hint that the NHL has a long way to go before it gets to Kim Davis's ideals of transparency and being that "North Star."

Let's rewind to the birth of the Hockey Diversity Alliance (HDA), which was forged by leading NHL and women players of color under the leadership of Akim Aliu but done outside of the purview of the league. It's not to be confused with the league's Player Inclusion Coalition.

Once you know Akim Aliu's story, it's easy to see why he's devoted himself to tearing hockey's old structures down, in order to build a new, better one in its place.

"It's funny; I have a love-hate relationship with this game," said Aliu on a cold autumn morning in 2022, as the HDA held an outdoor outreach event for kids in an overlooked Toronto neighborhood. "I love it to the deepest of my core, but there are times that I hate it just as much. It's really hard to stick with a sport that you've given everything to—mentally, physically, emotionally—but it doesn't always give the same thing back. But at the end of day, my thinking has changed. It's not really about me anymore, it's about the next generation. I'm hoping to pave a smoother path so they don't have to face the issues that the members of the HDA went through. So that's what it's all about for me, giving back to the next generation and hoping they have a smoother path."

Akim's globe-trotting family came to Canada from Ukraine. Aliu was born in the Nigerian metropolis of Lagos before moving to Kyiv. His father first came to Ukraine from Nigeria as an exchange student, then met his future wife at school. His family eventually relocated to Toronto, where Akim quickly excelled in the minor-hockey ranks. His family didn't have a lot of money, but minor-hockey teams would waive many of the fees in order to get Aliu to play for them.[1]

Aliu played top-level junior hockey in Ontario. The *Elite Prospects* site, an internationally followed scouting resource, stated that as "a very aggressive defenseman/winger, Aliu has excellent agitating qualities. He likes to hit and play a physical game. Also has some offensive ability and a quick release."[2]

For generations, elite hockey teams have embarked in hazing rituals, where rookies are "initiated" into the team by being victims of pranks or being forced to perform humiliating tasks. In 2005–06, his first year in the OHL, Aliu was with the Windsor Spitfires. Aliu's white teammates on the Spitfires gave him the racially derogatory nickname "eight-ball," for the black ball on a pool table.[3]

Aliu was still new to the Spitfires when the rookies on the team were ordered by the veterans to strip, and then be locked in the bathroom with the heat turned up. Aliu eventually forced his way out of the hazing prison. He was told by the vets to go back in and serve his time, but he said no.

His refusal did not go down well with the veterans. During a practice early in the 2005–06 season, eighteen-year-old winger Steve Downie, without provocation or warning, cross-checked the sixteen-year-old Aliu in the face. Then Downie started to throw punches. Aliu fought back to protect himself but, in the end, lost seven of his teeth—it was a brazen message that Aliu, a rookie and the only Black player on the Spitfires, did not have the right to say no to a humiliating hazing ritual.[4]

The incident became a viral video and hit the national news. Downie was suspended for five games, traded to the Peterborough Petes, and told to undergo professional counseling. But Aliu was also suspended—a one-game ban for defending himself. The OHL issued a $35,000 fine to the team. This is significant because the maximum fine in the OHL at the time was $25,000—so the league broke it down into two fines so it could break its own self-imposed maximum. Moe Mantha Jr., who was the head coach and general manager of the Spitfires, and was a former professional with twelve seasons in the NHL, received a twenty-five-game suspension from coaching and was not allowed to return as general manager of the Spitfires for one year. Mantha ended up leaving the team.

"I conclude that the lack of leadership and what transpired were dishonorable and prejudicial to the well-being of the League and its players," said OHL Commissioner David Branch as he levied the fines and suspension.

In May of 2006, Downie was signed by the Philadelphia Flyers and played about eleven and a half seasons in the NHL, signing million-dollar contracts with the Tampa Bay Lightning and the Colorado Avalanche. He was also known for his aggressive play, notching over one thousand minutes in penalties, and was suspended for twenty games for trying to deliberately injure Ottawa Senator Dean McAmmond in a preseason game.

Mantha was away from the game for a couple of years after the Downie/ Aliu incident but later continued his coaching career in junior hockey, including time with another OHL club.

Aliu's hockey career took a different path. In his autobiography, he admitted that, somehow, the hockey establishment blamed him for the Downie incident—that Aliu was the troublemaker. "Yet, despite my growing numbers and accolades…after the Downie incident, there was always this aura lingering around me that I was a bad kid."[5]

Aliu's draft stock plummeted, and he went No. 56 overall to the Chicago Blackhawks.

After graduating from the major junior ranks to the pros, Aliu was sent to a minor-league team to gain experience. It's exceptionally rare for a player to go right from the amateur ranks to the NHL, unless he's taken with one of the top-ten picks in the first round of the draft. Aliu was not a first-rounder.

The Blackhawks' farm team was the Rockford IceHogs, coached by Bill Peters. Rockford is only eighty miles from Chicago, but to players waiting for the call-up, they may as well have been playing on Mars. Getting from the minors is the toughest step of all; a player has worked so hard throughout his career to get to this point, but he's never sure that the final step will be taken.

Peters was an up-and-coming coach in the hockey world. He had apprenticed under famed coach Mike Babcock, who had gotten his name on the Stanley Cup as the coach of the Detroit Red Wings and led the Canadian men's national team to Olympic gold…twice. Babcock later coached the Toronto Maple Leafs. But while Babcock was a celebrity coach—seen by many in the hockey world as a master motivator—there were voices on social media, like former NHLer Mike Commodore, who labeled Babcock's leadership tactics as abusive. The Leafs fired Babcock in 2019, and he was exiled from the league for a period—he went back to the Canadian university level to coach. In 2023, he was brought in to coach the Columbus Blue Jackets but never got behind the bench for even a preseason game before he stepped down. An uproar was caused over reports he'd asked players for access to their smartphones. For a young player or any pro "on the bubble," a coach is seen as someone who has the ability to keep you in the NHL, dispatch you to the minors, or cut you outright. It's intimidating when he asks to go through your personal belongings.

After the *Spittin' Chiclets* podcast openly lambasted Babcock for his conduct, the NHL launched an investigation it would never have to finish. Soon after the NHL started looking into the phone affair, Babcock stepped down. His comeback effort finished in self-destruction.

Babcock and Peters had met when they were very green coaches, just beginning their careers at Red Deer College in central Alberta.

"I've known Mike for a long time, since Red Deer College back in 1988," Peters told me nearly a decade ago. "I was twenty-three, he was twenty-five. We've known each other's families for a long time—there's a friendship there as well as a professional relationship."[6]

(Full disclosure: I wrote a profile of Peters, one that was very complimentary of him, back in 2015. The reason I footnote my own work is not out of hubris but to be transparent with the reader about my own warts.)

With that résumé, Peters was on the fast track to the NHL. For Peters, Rockford was the final minor-league stop before getting his shot in the NHL.

But out of the public's sight, the dressing room in Rockford was in turmoil. Peters used the n-word in the dressing room. He criticized Aliu's choice in music. And maybe worst of all, because of Peters's criticisms, the Blackhawks' management believed Aliu was a problem player. Akim was sent down to lower minor-league teams—playing for the likes of the Toledo Walleye and the Gwinnett Gladiators. While these teams were located in the United States, and drivable from Chicago and Rockford, he might as well have been a world away.

When you're an up-and-coming player, the thing you fear the most is that coaches will spread the word that you are not a good teammate—that you are a "cancer" in the dressing room. And Aliu already had to wrestle with the stigma that the Downie incident was somehow *his* fault. So the prospect of coming forward, when a player sees his chances at his NHL career slipping away, that's just not an option when one is up against the culture.

It's one thing to be too intimidated to call out that uncle for his racist behavior at the Christmas dinner table, but it's another thing to call out an influential coach, who can wreck your career with one phone call to the parent team's general manager. In the dressing room, the power structure is far more oppressive than in an average workplace or social setting. In a sport where team chemistry is lauded as a major part of a winning formula, even a whiff of dissent can disastrously impact a player's stock.

The hockey community is smaller than you think; once a player gets a reputation as a bad apple, whether warranted or not, it's almost impossible to change people's minds. At the professional level, the coaches, general managers, and team presidents all know one another—so, even if you move to another team, it's difficult to earn a truly fresh start. The stories about you, whether true or not, follow you around. As of the end of February 2024, sixteen of the league's thirty-two head coaches had been previously behind the bench for other teams. While coaching is a job where the cliché "hired to get fired" truly applies, there is job security in the sense that once someone is done in one city, he can reappear in another. Coaches are constantly recycling—but not reinventing—themselves. So old ideas and old stigmas remain.

Aliu ended up only playing seven career NHL games, all with the Calgary Flames. He went on to play in Russia, Sweden, Slovakia, and Czechia.

While Aliu toiled in obscurity, Peters moved to the NHL. He was hired to coach the Carolina Hurricanes in 2014 and moved to the Calgary Flames in 2018. As Aliu's career diminished, Peters went on to bigger and better things.

But in 2019, with his NHL dreams in the rearview mirror, Akim made the decision to break his silence, telling the world about what happened to him in Rockford. This was corroborated by some of his former Rockford teammates. And then, former Carolina Hurricane player Michal Jordán went on social media and announced that, during his time with the team, Peters physically abused players. Jordán alleged that Peters kicked him and struck him in the back of the head during games.[7] The NHL opened an investigation. Later that year, Peters resigned as coach of the Flames, admitting that Aliu had told the truth.

But there was, and continues to be, a problem with the apology that Peters made the day he resigned from his job as the Flames' head coach. He wrote a letter of apology and addressed it to his boss, then–Calgary Flames general manager Brad Treliving.

"Please accept this as a sincere apology to you, and the entire Calgary Flames organization, for offensive language I used in a professional setting a decade ago," began the letter from Peters. "I know that my comments have been the source of both anger and disappointment, and I understand why. Although it was an isolated and immediately regrettable incident, I take responsibility for what I said."

The way the letter begins is reflective of how racism is often downplayed or swept under the rug in the game of hockey. First, it's not addressed to the people that Peters insulted and demeaned. It's addressed to his white boss. He referred to the "incident" without actually going into details about what he did. He never mentioned Aliu by name, and this letter never included an apology *to* Aliu.

This is another sign of how powerful the culture of hockey remains. There's a key edict you hear over and over as a player, and the media do not challenge it. It is a golden rule. It's "what happens in the room, stays in the room." That's why Peters could issue as vague an apology as a person in his position could make—and a lot of white journalists and movers and shakers would be satisfied by it.

Sure, a lot of people will say that Peters eventually paid for what happened in Rockford by losing his NHL coaching career. But Aliu already had his career derailed while others like Downie and Peters had very successful hockey careers. And maybe that should have been acknowledged by the now-former Flames coach.

There's an epilogue to the Peters story. As of 2023, he was back in the North American coaching ranks. After his exile in Russia, where he coached in the KHL, he's now behind the bench for the Lethbridge Hurricanes of the Western Hockey League (WHL), where he's stewarding the paths for teenage prospects.

But Aliu wasn't done. A perfect storm was coming. In 2020, much of the world was locked down, or at least had some of their movements restricted, thanks to the COVID pandemic. Sports leagues around the world postponed or canceled games. We were living in a world without any real distractions outside of COVID fears. We didn't have events to go to, didn't have to go out to the arena, theater, or restaurant. And with the world on pause, we had much more time to ponder a viral video of George Floyd.

This might be the unpopular opinion of the decade, but the reason Floyd's murder became a flash point, when the deaths of so many other Black victims at the hands of law enforcement came and went, was that sports wasn't on TV. We didn't have that reassurance that somewhere, somehow, sports leveled the playing field of life. Without the distraction, would we have paid more attention to the deaths of Black teens in America, or the hundreds of murdered or missing Indigenous women in Canada?

Aliu led the formation of the Hockey Diversity Alliance, which promotes inclusion in the game. The movement was sparked by Aliu's charges that institutional racism derailed his promising hockey career. BIPOC NHL players joined with BIPOC women's national-team-caliber players. Players of color, even those who had successful NHL careers, began to speak out. Major sponsors such as Scotiabank jumped on board.

While players appear in front of cameras and talk to reporters regularly, NHL players, and the teams themselves, are not as open with the public as NBA, NFL, or baseball teams. NBA stars will often talk about social issues, but hockey players rarely do. As the HDA was being formed, NFL players were kneeling during the national anthem to protest systemic racism in the United States.

That's why what Aliu and the HDA did was so necessary.

But the HDA isn't just about players opening up about racism in the game; the organization wants to launch grassroots programs that have an effect on the game as a whole. Advocacy is one part of what the HDA does; but another big part is ensuring more kids of color have the opportunity to play hockey, and that their first experiences in the game will be positive.

"Many people had their wake-up moments," said Edward Aliu, Akim's brother and the executive director of the HDA.

These stories show just how difficult inclusion and integration have been for the NHL. There's an old-school guard that's unwilling to change. There are marketing departments that quietly understand that the arena has been a white fortress for decades, a place for white fans to cheer on white players, a place that's stuck in time while other sports have tried to move forward.

In 2020, NHL Vice President of Diversity and Inclusion Kim Davis made this proclamation on the Black Girl Hockey Club video series: "How many season ticket holders are we willing to lose because we stand for something that is different than what we've articulated in the past? We have to be willing to lose some fans in order to gain some new ones."[8]

Culling the "bad" fans isn't easy, though. Imagine a game of Whac-A-Mole that includes both professional and grassroots arenas, social media, traditional media, and fans who gather at bars to watch games.

IT STARTS WHEN THEY ARE YOUNG

Find a map of Saskatchewan and place your finger as close as you can to the middle of it. Chances are it will end up pretty close to the dot that represents Prince Albert.

It's officially a city (in Canada, any center that has more than ten thousand people is designated a "city") but feels more like a small town. It has fewer than forty thousand people living in it—barely enough to fill two NHL arenas.

This is where Matt Dumba first learned to skate—about a fifteen-hour drive northwest of the Twin Cities, where he'd really make his mark as an NHL player.

His dad, Charle, is white. His mom, Treena, is Filipino. But the diversity in the Dumba family goes much deeper than that. Matt grew up in Prince Albert with aunts and uncles of different races. His mom was adopted into a large family, with eight brothers and sisters who were of varying backgrounds. Black. White. Indigenous. Asian.

To Dumba, being part of a diverse family unit wasn't anything his young brain would register as unusual. But once he began playing minor hockey, Dumba was confronted with racism—and realized that both the color of his skin and his family background were going to be used against him.

"I didn't understand it with my family," recalled Dumba. "It wasn't until I faced racism, growing up, in hockey, that I got a better understanding of how unique my family situation was. I didn't understand what it meant to be in a family that was a cultural mosaic."

Racial slurs became part of his everyday life at the rink. When he was eight, his family moved to Calgary, and he played in the Crowchild Minor Hockey Association. From there, he would play major junior hockey with the Red Deer Rebels of the Western Hockey League, about a ninety-minute drive from Calgary. He was named the WHL's rookie of the year in 2010–11, and he was the seventh-overall draft pick in 2012, selected by the Wild. He played for Canada at the 2014 World Junior Championships and won gold with the national team at the 2016 World Championships. In 2018, he signed a five-year extension with the Wild, worth $30 million USD. He bet on himself and signed a one-year, $3.9 million deal with the Arizona Coyotes in 2023, knowing that he'd be going to a losing team, but he was putting himself in the shop window for a better long-term deal later on. He was traded to the Tampa Bay Lightning in 2024 and then signed a two-year, $7.5 million USD contract with the Dallas Stars on July 1, 2024.

While he's now a star defenseman in the NHL, he said racism is still a problem in minor hockey across North America—and not enough is being done to change things. "I think the biggest barrier was how often I dealt with racial taunts, slurs, guys trying to get under your skin," said Matt. "I dealt with that on a pretty regular basis. And it wasn't just from the other teams, a lot of the time, my own teams, too. It's tough because little kids are the biggest culprits of it all, because they are naive and ignorant."

The point is this: It might be easy to think that there are stories of players who overcome racism and became star players (like Dumba) and that we have a very neat and tidy happy ending. But the point is simple; there is no such thing as a player of color who can escape racism just because he or she is pretty darn good.

Even today, Dumba believes that minor-hockey associations aren't doing enough to handle hockey's issues with race. He said that if you put him in charge of a minor-hockey association, he'd create a rule that when a family first enrolls a child in the sport, racial sensitivity training would need to be completed before that kid was allowed to set a skate on the ice. Learning to respect teammates and opponents would be just as important as how to take powerful strides and how to shoot a puck.

But Dumba doesn't think the sensitivity training should just be given to the kids—the adults need it, too. Actually, the adults likely need it more.

"They should start out when kids first begin hockey, and there should be different levels of educational programs that you have to go through when you first register for hockey," said Dumba. "And this needs to be something we see across the country. And I don't think that only the kids should be taking it—this should be something for everyone at the rink, whether you are volunteering to coach or you're reffing. Someone or something has to take control of this, to show that there's no tolerance for racism. It's about how we police the game and how we react to racially charged incidents."

And if a kid, parent, or official is found to be spreading racist views at the rink, Dumba believes not only the punishments need to be harsh, but also the offender will need to pass several tests before that person is let back into the arena.

"There have to be suspensions, and then further steps you go through to get back into the game," he said. "This game is a privilege. No one should have the right to play hockey. I was lucky enough to have that privilege when I was younger. It took a village to get me through it, and I am so thankful that they did. I had good friends and family around me. And that's the best part of the game; it's the friendships that you build. We're not all going to make the NHL; that's just the facts. And some of the guys who didn't make it, they're still some of my best friends. We still have those memories of playing on those outdoor rinks, playing mini sticks in hallways and, well, just being kids. I just hope one day that all kids across the board have those same opportunities.

"It also comes down to the education of the parents, too, and everyone involved in the game—the refs, the scorers' box, people working at the arena, it needs to be all hands on deck. This stuff should not still be happening."

In 2019, USA Hockey made a rule change—affecting all leagues under its purview. Before the change, any player who used abusive or racist language on the ice would receive a game misconduct. But as then president Jim Smith wrote in an open letter to American hockey families, it did little to stop abusive acts. "For reasons which I cannot explain or understand, this penalty does not seem to be enough of a deterrent to stop this conduct," Smith wrote.

So, USA Hockey upped the ante. The rule as it stands now: if a player utters abusive language, a match penalty is assessed. A match penalty is more severe than a game misconduct because it compels a league to have a hearing and consider supplementary discipline. And the offending player can't come back to play until the league makes a ruling—and that hearing has to happen within thirty days of the offense.

The Canadian Hockey League (CHL), which oversees the three major junior hockey circuits in Canada and the United States—which are basically prep league for future pros—issued this statement in 2020:

> It remains clear that the topic of race, inequity, and discrimination in our society is something we all need to address. Sports are not immune to these critical issues, and as leaders in our communities we have the opportunity to use our platforms to help be a voice for systemic change.
>
> The Canadian Hockey League, together with our regional leagues the Western Hockey League, Ontario Hockey League and Quebec Major Junior Hockey League are united in our commitment to building inclusive environments for our players, teams, staff, and fans. It is important that we all do our part to reinforce the message that everyone should be treated fairly and equally, regardless of race.[9]

In early 2022, those words were tested. The Ontario Hockey League didn't settle at suspending Terry Christensen, who had been the president of the Flint Firebirds. The decision was made to kick him out of the league. "His conduct violated the League's expectation of the appropriate conduct of a representative of an OHL team and he has lost the privilege to participate in the League," read the league's statement.[10]

While the league itself never revealed the nature of the complaint that led to Christensen's expulsion, reports emerged that it was due to alleged racial comments aimed at a player on the team.

In the sport of hockey, Christensen's case is far from an isolated one, but it remains one of the few cases where the punishment fit the crime. For the most part, we've seen hockey leagues, from the junior ranks all the way to the pros, struggle when it comes to policing bigotry. Sure, they know what to do when a player delivers a check from behind or starts a brawl, but often, racism is met with little more than lip service.

In the previous chapter, Courtney Szto spoke of the need to educate coaches, parents, and kids about the racially charged history of the sport. Why not take that further?

"For those who would like the power to teach children, to officiate or work in administrative roles, anti-racism education should be part of the price of admission," said Szto. "For parents and players, I believe that anti-racism or anti-oppression education should be optional, but be made readily accessible."[11]

Dumba said he knows a player of color who used to play in the NHL and is now looking at how his kid will be treated in minor hockey. It's caused a crisis of conscience.

"His kid is going into hockey understanding that this is something very real that they have to experience, and most likely will," said Dumba. "Do you want to put your kid in hockey, still? Are they going to love it, and get a good experience from it? That's up in the air for kids of color. That's not fair. Simple as that. Parents come up to me and, oh man, they pour their hearts out, with tears and stuff. They're telling me that they didn't understand what they were doing to their kids by putting them into hockey, and the hardships that would ensue from it. And there's the white parent [of mixed kids] or the adoptive parent, and they don't have the full understanding of what their child is going through because he's a different color. Those stories just touch you, and they give you motivation to be pursuing this and sticking with this and staying relevant. It's a brutal stain on the game I love."

Think about it. Here we have an NHL player, signed to a multimillion-dollar contract, a man who has played for his country in international tournaments, and he's openly wondering if hockey is the right sport for kids of color. He's wondering if the costs of getting to the top of the ladder, the racist insults and discrimination a player will face along the way, is worth it. If that's not enough to get your attention, maybe nothing will.

Georges Laraque was one of the most beloved tough guys in NHL history. He delivered punishing hits on the ice, and opposing players feared having to face him. He played in the Quebec Major Junior Hockey League and was drafted by the Edmonton Oilers. Laraque played 695 NHL games with the Oilers, Pittsburgh Penguins, Phoenix Coyotes, and Montreal Canadiens.

After his playing days came to an end, he's taken on a variety of roles; he's a motivational speaker and a radio host, and he's even dabbled in politics with the Green Party of Canada. Off the ice, you could not wipe the smile from his face. His love of hockey was infectious.

Considering how he began his hockey journey in Montreal, it might be a minor miracle that he even kept playing into his teens, let alone make it all the way to the NHL. He recalled that he was subjected to abuse, not from just one or two parents or opposing players, but from large groups of people. Entire groups of fans would unite and shout racial epithets at him.

When he was nine years old, his parents wouldn't go to any more of his minor-hockey games and wanted him to quit playing the sport. They were sick and tired of hearing the N-word chanted in the Montreal rinks in which their son played.

But Laraque didn't quit. He decided to persevere, to stick to a game that didn't return to him the same sort of love that he poured into it. Game after game, racial slurs were tossed at him on the ice and chanted in the stands. "They thought, 'what kid could endure that?'" Laraque said. "But they underestimated my strength."

He kept playing, but it was a solitary journey. He was alone within a team game.

"You hear a lot of stories about players who are supported by their parents as they played minor hockey. That was not my story," said Laraque. "But I told my parents I didn't care, I wanted to prove people wrong. In minor hockey, the kids are saying the things that their parents are teaching them. And it was hurtful."

To keep playing hockey without his parents' support, Georges paid for his registration and equipment by shoveling driveways and mowing lawns. He'd find used equipment. Sticks were expensive, so, when he broke one, he taped it back together.

"I knew I couldn't take a slap shot," he said.

By the time he was fifteen, Laraque had the chance to play soccer, football, or hockey at elite levels. Football or soccer would be an easier path for a Black athlete, but he chose hockey.

In 1992, Laraque made his debut in the Quebec Major Junior Hockey League with the St. Jean Lynx. He was drafted by the Oilers in 1995 and made his NHL debut in the 1997–98 season. Being a tough guy in the NHL usually means a long, indirect path to the NHL, with lots of seasoning in the minor leagues. Laraque used the racism he faced throughout his life as emotional fuel.

"I didn't just want to be another player, I wanted to be a role model," said Georges. "Hockey is a white man's sport, but I wanted to show that racism could not stop me."

This echoes the experiences of Val James, who, in the 1981–82 season, became the first Black American to play in the NHL. Before James got to the NHL, though, he packed up and left his home on Long Island so he could play higher-level junior hockey in Canada. First, he was in Midland, Ontario, a small city north of Toronto that is one of the gateways to Great Lakes cottage country. Then, he went to Quebec City, where he played for the Remparts. His experiences were similar to Laraque's, even though James was trying to break into the game at a time when you could still count the number of professional players of color on one hand.

In his autobiography, James discussed how hard it was for white team-mates to relate to how isolated he felt. No matter how sympathetic his white teammates were, they just couldn't understand racism at its most base level, because it didn't happen to them. Sure, witnessing it is one thing, but feeling its sting is another.

It is something that I, the author of this book, am still just beginning to see. It wasn't until after I got married, and my wife and I had mixed-race children, that I could really even begin to understand racism at a deeper level. And even as my kids grow older, I would never dare suggest that I *understand* it. I see it, I get enraged by it, but at worst it's one degree of separation from me.

"Of course, when I was subjected to racial abuse on road trips, I could count on the support of my teammates," James wrote. "They always said the right things, but try as they may, they couldn't really sympathize with what I was going through. An old Midland teammate recently brought up an incident when opposing fans threw bananas at me. What the hell could my fellow teenagers on the Flyers say to make that better? They would be offended on my behalf, but not being Black themselves, they just could not relate to the pain and humiliation and anger that I was experiencing. In that sense, I was very much alone."[12]

"When I got to the NHL, I thought about my journey," said Georges. "I dedicated my hockey career to everyone who called me names."

For players who experience racism at the arena, the love of the game is slowly eroded. And for a player who is good at hockey, who has gotten to the level where they are too good to simply walk away and quit the game for good, one of the best ways to cope is to start seeing the game not as something fun to do but as work.

That was how it was for Saroya Tinker. She's now the manager of diversity, equity, and inclusion initiatives and community engagements for the Professional Women's Hockey League, which began play in 2024. Before that, she played pro hockey for the Toronto Six, and she's represented Canada at the junior level. She grew up in Oshawa, a suburb just east of Toronto, and she remembers that when she played at an elite level in the Durham West minor-hockey system, she fell out of love with hockey.

"I always say that I played angry. I think I kept a lot of it inside. It was a job. I put my headphones in, I did my job at the arena and left," Saroya remembered. "They say hockey is for everyone, but not everyone is welcomed. We see BIPOC individuals being pushed out from an early age. I would say there has been movement since I was young, but, still, there's a long way to go."

She was in a shell because, when she told her coaches about racism at the arena, they didn't listen. It is so hard for a player to come forward because often the victim is blamed. A player who complains about racism is often told not to cause problems on the team. They didn't cause the trouble, but yet, by speaking out, they're seen as the troublemakers. They are the outsiders.

Tinker didn't feel like her teammates had her back.

"I think there's always been a lack of accountability, whether it was me bringing up issues in the dressing room and telling my coach and him not doing anything about it, or my teammates not sticking up or saying something if they heard a racial slur," said Saroya. "I think, all in all, it's about accountability. There needs to be consequences, and there needs to be education on how to deal with these issues. We actually need to implement and force the issues.

"We need those uncomfortable conversations to be had. And the uncomfortable conversations have to come from our allies, too. We're aware those are the higher-ups, those who are running our organizations. If they're not having the uncomfortable conversations and educating themselves, we're not going to get anywhere. We talk about allyship, and I think the white individuals need to learn how to be true allies."

While Tinker, Dumba, and Laraque faced overt, out-in-the-open bigotry at the rink, we have to understand that racism is multifaceted. Racism is something a lot of white people (including myself, till I started doing the research for this book) equate with burning crosses and brown shirts and marches in places like Charlottesville. But racism is also institutional, and it can be subtle—so much so that the white majority that made the rules in the first place can't see it. Racism is also about recognizing that the very institutions we work in were created by whites, and that the rule books were written by whites.

Think about the equipment that players wear. There are no allowances for those outside the traditional cultural hockey norm. The Indo-Canadian community is mad about hockey, so much so that *Hockey Night in Canada* launched a simulcast in Punjabi back in 2008, and they are still going strong in the present day.

But there are barriers for Sikhs, where hockey becomes a battle between their faith and identity, and their love of the game. For a Sikh male, the turban is more than a symbol—it's a part of his identity. But as a teenage prospect who was showing that he was ready to move to the elite ranks, Arshdeep Bains was forced to make a choice. To keep playing hockey at a high level, he'd need to wear the same type of helmet that pretty well everyone else in the elite ranks wore—and that didn't allow the room needed to fit religious headwear under it.

When Arshdeep started playing hockey, putting on a helmet wasn't easy. That's because as a Sikh, he wore a *patka* (a kind of turban worn by Sikh boys) to cover his hair. His two older brothers, Amrit and Harvir, also had to wear oversized helmets to cover their religious headwear. Those big helmets announced to the world that they were different.

After leading the Western Hockey League in scoring in 2021–22, he signed with his hometown Vancouver Canucks in 2022. When I spoke to him, he was plying his trade with the team's top minor-league affiliate in nearby Abbotsford, British Columbia. In February of 2024, he made his NHL debut with the Canucks. On October 27, 2024, in a game against the Pittsburgh Penguins on *Hockey Night in Canada*, Bains potted his first NHL goal.

Bains's father came to Canada from India and fell in love with Wayne Gretzky and the powerful Oilers team that dominated hockey through the 1980s. He pushed his sons toward playing minor hockey. (Arshdeep's dad has since then become a Canucks fan.)

"I had older brothers who played, and I heard about some of the challenges they had," said Arshdeep. "We used to wear turbans, and that can be hard to mix into hockey, to have under your helmet. Being looked at differently, for sure I've seen that, and, back to the turban part, when you wear it to the rink, it's pretty obvious you're different from anyone else. Your hair is longer, your helmet is bigger, and you get name-called and stuff like that. I'm sure it happened to them, it happened to me."

When he realized he was good enough to play high-level junior hockey, he knew, for both safety and performance reasons, he'd have to make a tough decision.

"I took my turban off and cut my hair when I got to Bantam," said Bains. "That's what I felt I had to do to play in junior, to fit in, and it also helped with the visor. There's a bit of sacrifice you have to do, there. It was more to do with the helmet. I needed to make sure the helmet fit properly. I was becoming a pretty good hockey player, and I knew if I wanted to play in the Western League, I knew [the big helmet] wasn't going to work."

Courtney Szto's book, *Changing on the Fly: Hockey Through the Voices of South Asian Canadians*, opens with a story that came from when she was a young staffer at a Sport Chek outlet.[13] A Sikh family asked for her help in finding hockey equipment for their young son. When a helmet that comfortably fit over his patka could not be found, the family left the store, a pile of equipment left behind as a reminder of how hard it is for those of the Sikh faith to find accommodation in the game.

ON THE ICE

Ohio State and Michigan State. Their basketball and football rivalries have been cemented over decades and decades of games. Michigan State is also a traditional hockey power. Nearly eighty players who have skated for the Spartans have gone onto NHL careers; TNT and Sportsnet hockey analyst Anson Carter, and Carolina Hurricanes coach Rod Brind'Amour are Michigan State alumni.

Jagger Joshua hopes to join in that tradition. His older brother, Dakota, has already realized the dream of playing in the NHL; he plays for the Vancouver Canucks.

But in 2022, Jagger got a lesson at how poorly racism is handled at the collegiate level—and it got to the point where Joshua stepped in.

On November 11, 2022, the Michigan State Spartans faced the Ohio State Buckeyes on the ice. An Ohio State player, Kamil Sadlocha, received a game misconduct in the second period. After the game, Jagger took to social media to let his followers know that he was repeatedly targeted by an Ohio State player during the game—with racial slur after racial slur. He didn't name the player, but said the Buckeye who hurled the insults got a misconduct.

Now, when I write "after the game," I don't mean that he was in the dressing room on his iPhone, just minutes after the final. It took *days*. At first, Joshua didn't say much, but then he took to social media because he was stunned that there was no follow-up discipline from the Big Ten Conference, even though officials from the conference had launched an investigation into the incident. He waited and waited for a ruling, but when nothing came, that's when he decided to go public.

"The inaction has left me feeling confused and pessimistic about the movement of diversity within hockey culture," Jagger posted. "The ignorance of racism does not belong in our game, and I feel that I need to make people aware that this incident occurred, because, without acknowledgement, the problem gets worse."

After the statement, fans put two and two together. Since Sadlocha was the only player in the game to receive a misconduct, he must have been the player Joshua was talking about.

After Jagger went public, Ohio State suspended Sadlocha. The team sent the Polish forward home. Gene Smith, the athletic director at Ohio State, issued a public apology to Jagger. Smith pledged that the whole Ohio State team would undergo racial sensitivity training. "No student or student-athlete should experience hatred or racism, and everyone should feel welcome," Smith wrote as part of his apology to Joshua.

Dakota weighed in on his brother's situation. Speaking to reporters in the Canucks' dressing room, he said that "it's a terrible situation to be a part of. But his goal is to put it out there so people can learn from it and hope it doesn't happen again.

"You would like to think we've come a long way, especially over recent years, but obviously [this] still keeps happening. So, until it's nonexistent, I don't think it's surprising."

A month after the incident, Sadlocha was allowed to return to the Buckeyes.

Top players from junior leagues and American colleges, along with top under-twenty players from European leagues, can be selected to play for their national teams at the World Junior Championships. This is where fans can get a sneak preview of who are going to be the star NHL players of the future. In Canada, the World Juniors, regularly held during the Christmas season, is one of the biggest TV events of the year. When Canada hosts the tournament, it is played in NHL-size arenas that, outside of the COVID epidemic, sell out. In Canada, it is the Final Four and the Rose Bowl rolled into one.

The gold-medal game of the 2020 World Juniors was a classic. Canada and Russia were tied 3–3 late in the third period, but Akil Thomas stormed into the Russian zone and slammed the puck in the net to give the Canadians a lead they wouldn't give up. But before Thomas earned the international spotlight, he endured racism in the very country he represented. He wore the red maple leaf on his jersey, but Canadian hockey culture had not always been good to him.

Thomas was selected to play major junior hockey by the Niagara Ice-Dogs, a team that plays its home games in the city of St. Catharines, Ontario. That city is just a short drive away from the American border.

When a player gets picked by one of the major junior teams, he needs to find a place to live. This isn't easy when you are a teenager. So, teams find billets—these are families who let the players stay with them. A lot of players will see the billets as a second family.

In an interview with Anson Carter for NBC Sports, Thomas talked about what it was like in his first year of junior—and that what was supposed to be his second home wasn't so welcoming. "My billet dad would kind of get drunk sometimes and kind of told me that he was the most racist guy I'll ever meet," Akil said. "That was tough. It was a whole experience, and I didn't want to tell anyone at the time because I was a sixteen-year-old and I didn't want to draw attention to myself. I just wanted to focus on hockey."[14]

He moved away from that billet after that first season.

It's difficult for players of color to reconcile playing for their country, when they're often mistreated in that very nation. And some, like Saroya Tinker, find that their memories of playing internationally are tainted by what they see as inaction about racial issues in hockey at home.

"For myself, I was lucky enough to put the Team Canada jersey on some years ago," said Tinker. "Honestly, it's a huge honor. But at this point in time, I think, we're getting back to conversations about accountability in the hockey community. I think there's a lack of accountability, and we see that in our higher-ups. Things need to change. I don't think that we're on the right track. I don't think the right answers have been given."

Not on the right track, after we've seen so many platitudes about change in the game? She's got a point. Proof? I am going to ask you to put down this book. Once you do, turn on your smartphone or laptop, and type "racism" and "minor hockey" into a Google search. Then, join me again.

(Waiting. Waiting. Waiting.)

How many examples did you find? It will differ depending on where you are in the world. Here's what I found, in the basement of my home in Edmonton. The first three hits of my Google search were: A family made claims of racial abuse in a suburban Vancouver minor-hockey league;[15] a Toronto teenager said he is thinking about quitting hockey after hearing racial slurs on the ice;[16] a player in Gatineau, Quebec opened up about the racism he faced.[17]

In 2021, the Angus Reid Institute, which is a Canadian nonprofit organization that polls people on everything from what they like to eat to whom they plan to vote for in the next election, conducted a survey about the game of hockey. Angus Reid asked Canadians how they felt about the game. When it came to the topics of racism and exclusion, the verdicts were harsh. Half of those who answered the poll said that hockey as a whole has some problem with racism. Only 18 percent said they don't feel hockey has any issues when it comes to racism.[18] The rest of those who answered were undecided.

For those who believe hockey doesn't have issue with race—or are undecided on the issue—allow me to present even more of the more infamous cases from the past few years. I am not pulling examples from twenty or thirty years ago—these are incidents that are happening in rinks across North America in the present day.

Mark Connors, a Black goalie, was sixteen when he made headlines across Canada. Connors's team was based in Nova Scotia and participated in a November 2021 tournament in nearby Charlottetown, Prince Edward Island. He was subjected to racial slurs not only on the ice but back at the hotel in which his team was staying. He came forward, and the incident was investigated by Hockey P.E.I. The result? Five players were each handed 25-game suspensions for their racist actions.

In its decision, Hockey P.E.I.'s disciplinary committee stated: "A lengthy suspension is required in order to reflect the seriousness of this type of conduct and to recognize the degrading nature of racial slurs. A racial slur attacks the very core of what it means to be recognized as a person."[19]

But the fact that this happened at the rink, *and* at the hotel, shows just how easy it is to be comfortable with racism within hockey's culture.

Let's stay in Prince Edward Island. In December of 2021, Keegan Mitchell and his Sherwood Metros faced the Kensington Vipers in a Junior B game on the island. A Vipers' player uttered an anti-Asian slur at Mitchell's teammate. After the game, Hockey P.E.I. handed the player who uttered the insult a two-game suspension. Yup, you've already noticed that it's a radically different verdict than what was handed out to Connors's tormentors.

Mitchell decided it was time to say something. He thought the suspension wasn't tough enough. He took to Facebook and wrote these words:

"For those of you who know me personally or through hockey, I am almost absolutely certain you recognize me as someone who always stands up for themselves, but more importantly for my friends and teammates. If Hockey P.E.I. took these scenarios as seriously as they say they do, this player would have been suspended appropriately."

How did Hockey P.E.I. react? It handed Mitchell an indefinite suspension. For being critical of how the hockey organization was dealing with racism, Mitchell received a harsher penalty than the player who uttered the racist insult. Allyship isn't easy.

Thankfully, when the news of the suspension went out, public outrage went up. Way up. And Hockey P.E.I. felt the pressure. The story hit the major newspapers and Canadian sports networks. The organization was forced to end Mitchell's suspension, then issued this public apology:

"We acknowledge and express our sincere regret for errors that were made in our handling of the incident. This incident has made us realize that our inclusivity and anti-harassment guidelines for officials, teams, players and their families do not go far enough to protect those that they should. We are committed to changing not only the guidelines of the game on the island, but the culture as well. We can and will do better."

ONLINE WARRIORS

The NHL has created a zero-tolerance policy for slurs and abuse at the rinks, but policing the internet is an entirely different—and impossible— task. Hidden by the veil of anonymity, gatekeepers work overtime to make players of color feel loathed and threatened.

Social media has become society's most powerful tool for hate. And the so-called hockey "fans," the ones Davis said the NHL needs to be willing to jettison, are comfortable targeting players of color. It doesn't matter if they score game-winning goals or make game-altering mistakes, no matter if what they do on the ice hurts or helps their teams, every single action is a reason to be targeted.

Dumba said he does his best to stay away from social media. But no matter how much he tries to unplug from Twitter or Instagram, he can't 100 percent avoid it. NHL players are public figures, and often their teams feature them on their social media feeds. When he does go on social media, he has to brace himself.

"I don't have Instagram on my phone, I don't go on it that much," said Dumba. "But there was some stuff I had to do for the Wild, so I had that account open yesterday. And it [racism] was just everywhere. After every game, it's ridiculous, people hiding behind anonymous accounts, the direct messages you get, the tweets. It's kind of wild when you think about it. But part of me feels bad for these people—that they can just sit there and have so much hate in their hearts, and they think, 'Hey, it's OK for me to say that to this person, to another human. This is how I get my message across.' It's sad we have people like that in our world, who have that hate bottled up inside them for some reason."

Washington Capitals player Joel Ward was caught in the middle of an online racist firestorm during the 2012 Eastern quarter-final playoffs.

It's the dream for many kids who grow up in Canada—to score a series-winning goal. In overtime, to boot. It happened to Ward. But his story is different from most. It doesn't end with mass celebrations and fans toasting his name.

He and his teammates were in a do-or-die Game 7 with the defending Stanley Cup champion Boston Bruins. The deciding game, in Boston, was tied 1–1 heading into overtime. A couple of minutes into the extra frame, Ward pounced on a rebound in front of Bruins goaltender Tim Thomas and scored the series winner.

It's tradition for NHL teams to line up and shake hands at the end of a hard-fought playoff series. But after the teams honored that tradition, and the arena emptied, what followed was anything but sportsmanlike. Minutes after the Bruins were eliminated, social media was filled with racist messages aimed at Ward. It was inexcusable. But when awful things happen on social media, which feels like pretty much all the time, they snowball. One horrible post leads to another. Racism lurks behind the keyboards, and spreads via anonymous account after anonymous account.

The Bruins were forced to make a statement, condemning the so-called fans who were targeting the Capitals' series-winning scorer. "The Bruins are very disappointed by the racist comments that were made following the game last night. These classless, ignorant views are in no way a reflection of anyone associated with the Bruins organization."

For Ward, though, it was just another day in the NHL.

"As I got older, even playing in National Hockey League games, I'd be skating around the rink...and hear 'go back to Africa' 'go play basketball,'" he said.[20] "I've been called everything."

It's hard to find a silver lining in mass racist behavior. But Ward said the ugliness that followed his OT goal, and the fact it played out not behind closed doors but in front of NHL fans across North America led to a positive. He felt that finally, his teammates understood that it's not easy to be a BIPOC player in the NHL. The feeling of isolation that players of color feel in hockey's dressing room became just a little more obvious to the white majority.

"For my teammates, it was a learning curve. The stuff that I went through in 2012 in Boston, for people who wanted me dead for scoring a hockey goal, *come on*. To have conversations with my teammates, to have them understand, to me I took a big positive out of things."

Ethan Bear, a defenseman who grew up in Ochapowace Nation in Saskatchewan, realized a dream when he was selected by the Edmonton Oilers in the fifth round of the 2015 NHL draft. Players drafted in the lower rounds aren't expected to make it to the NHL; they're prospects who will need seasoning in the minor leagues, just for the chance to get a chance.

Yet, Bear played just eighty-nine games in the minor leagues before he solidified himself as a regular with the Oilers. And his Indigenous heritage was celebrated by the team. The Oilers even got permission from the NHL to put Bear's name in Cree lettering on the back of his jersey for a preseason game.

Sadly, the fairy tale quickly transformed into a horror story during the 2021 playoffs. The Oilers faced the Winnipeg Jets in the first round. The Oilers were heavy favorites going into the first round of the post-season, and with good reason. During the regular season, the Jets did not beat the Oilers.

But the series did not go well for Edmonton. Not only did the Oilers lose the series, they got swept. In the final game of that series, Bear was criticized for making a bad play that led to a Winnipeg goal. Now, Bear was far from the only Oiler to make mistakes on the ice. After all, the Oilers did not win a game in the series. Mistakes are part of the game. Wayne Gretzky made them. Mario Lemieux made them.

But on social media, Bear was subjected to racist posts. He became the poster boy for his team's failings.

Every NHL player is well aware that high pressure is part of the business. If they make mistakes, they will be criticized on TV broadcasts, in newspapers, and on websites. If the conversation sticks with hockey, they're fine with it. They understand that someone will point out a time when a player was out of position or made a bad pass. As players and coaches say over and over, "it's a results-oriented business." And when the results don't go your way, coaches get fired and players get traded, sent down to the minors, or cut.

Where they draw the line is when the criticism stops being about what happens on the ice and becomes personal.

In Bear's case, it was ugly.

"I felt like I lost us the whole series, the way people were treating me," Ethan said. "They made me the scapegoat, like, the reason why we lost. But I wasn't. It *was one play*. When I had all that, and you could see everything on social media, whether it's Twitter, Facebook, or Instagram, and all of it is racism. And then you get all these DMs. For myself, it was like, shocking that people would go so low."[21]

"For him to be pushed that far, it hurt so much," said Lloyd Bear, Ethan's father.

The Oilers released a statement. "The Edmonton Oilers Hockey Club is disappointed in these disgusting, cowardly and racist remarks. While we have witnessed progress in the area of equality and inclusion, this reprehensible behavior demonstrates we still have significant work to do. Ethan Bear is an incredibly skilled hockey player and a beloved teammate. His community-minded efforts both here in Edmonton and in Saskatchewan represent the qualities any organization could possibly ask of its members."

Despite the statement of support, Bear did not play another game for the Oilers. Before the next season began, he was traded to the Carolina Hurricanes. He returned to Edmonton in December 2021 as a member of the Hurricanes and was part of a 3–1 win.

"I've been thinking about it for a long time, ever since the trade happened," Bear said about coming back to Edmonton. "It's definitely something I've been waiting for, for a long time.

"When you come in here and think about all the negatives that happened at the end…I try to think of it [coming back to Edmonton] as a positive. I think about all the good memories I have from my time here, the coaching staff, the training staff, and some of the guys. I really did love playing here. But when I got traded because of everything that happened at the end, I wasn't sure if I should be happy or sad."

Bear was traded to the Vancouver Canucks in 2022, and, as a free agent, signed with the Washington Capitals late in 2023. Edmonton is the closest city to Bear's Ochapowace Nation home. And when he returned to the Alberta capital as a member of the Capitals in 2024, there was a group of

Indigenous fans gathered, holding signs that read "Bear Watcher." Representation matters. It absolutely does.

Later in 2024, Bear entered the player assistance program of the NHLPA (National Hockey League Players' Association) and NHL.

In April 2020, a hacker ruined an online event hosted by the New York Rangers as a way to introduce fans to first-round draft pick K'Andre Miller, a defenseman from the University of Wisconsin. While fans were on the Zoom call, a racial slur was repeated hundreds of times in the chat box.

The NHL released this statement: "The person who committed this despicable act is in no way an NHL fan and is not welcome in the hockey community.

"No one deserves to be subjected to such ugly treatment and it will not be tolerated in our league. We join with the Rangers in condemning this disgusting behavior."

Then Rangers veteran Jacob Trouba took to Twitter to condemn the action. "What happened today was inexcusable and cowardly. Racism has no place in the hockey community or the world."

The thing is, you can have allies who rush to a player of color's defense after the fact, there can be social media pronouncements that make public admonishments of racism, but how hard is it for a player to pull on a team's sweater, knowing that, somewhere, there are other fans with those replica jerseys who are spewing their hatred?

Nazem Kadri, currently with the Calgary Flames, has established himself as one of the grittiest forwards in modern hockey. The Lebanese Canadian winger plays the game with an edge, and, yes, there have been times when he's crossed the line. Kadri is never going to win the Lady Byng Trophy, which is handed out annually to the NHL's "most gentlemanly player." But that doesn't separate him from dozens of legendary forwards in NHL history. The late, great Gordie Howe played with an edge, too—in fact the hockey term "Gordie Howe hat trick" is a term given to a player who scores a goal, registers an assist, and gets in a fight in the same game.

Kadri scores goals, too—and in 2021–22, as a member of the Avalanche, he registered 87 points in 71 regular-season games.

But racist abuse came to the forefront in the 2022 playoffs.

In a series against St. Louis, Kadri collided with Blues goalie Jordan Binnington. On the play, Binnington was injured. Kadri had crashed the net, looking for a rebound, when he and a Blues defenseman collided; the trainwreck also took out the goalie. The NHL ruled that the play was not dirty, and that no suspension or discipline of any kind was warranted.

Before the collision with Binnington, Kadri had been suspended six times, including an incident from the 2021 playoffs against those same St. Louis Blues. With that kind of history, there is no doubt that, had the NHL bosses had any inkling that the play on Binnington was intentional, they would have thrown the book at Kadri. Still they did nothing.

But social media was filled with its own arbiters, and their judgments included torrents of hate aimed toward Kadri. There were spiteful, ignorant comments about his faith—Islam—and his heritage. He even received death threats.

"People need to be aware that this stuff still happens," Kadri said during the playoffs. "And it's hurtful. I know a lot of people don't have to deal with that, and they might not understand what it feels like. But people are trying [to fight racism], which I appreciate. But you know, at the end of the day, I'm a good hockey player and I just try to provide for my team and try to put all of that aside.

"I just worry about some people, some kids, that aren't as mentally tough as I am and have to go under it, through that scrutiny and that criticism. That's why I want to do the best I can to help."

Kadri not only got to hoist the Stanley Cup over his head at the end of the 2021–22 season, he got to share it with his family. An enduring image from the Avalanche's celebrations is of Kadri passing his father, Samir, the Cup. His family also got the chance to celebrate in London, Ontario, when Kadri was able to bring the Cup back to his hometown during the off-season.

Then there's the stuff that occurs out of public view, the hate that festers in the DMs.

Dumba said that if more players of color shared the nature of the insults they receive, most fans would be shocked. But they want to give their energies to solving the problems, rather than give airtime to the trolls who harass them.

"Honestly, if you ask any guy of color to screenshot some of his DMs after games, you'd see a lot of things said that would blow people's minds or whatever," said Dumba. "But we have to rise above that. There's ways to rise above this situation, and there are bigger and better things we can give our energy to, and that's helping kids across these countries [the US and Canada] rise above and believe in themselves. They need to be empowered to be themselves, no matter their race, religion, or gender."

HOW PRIDE WENT WRONG

When it comes to making themselves more open and welcoming to LGBTQ2S+ communities across North America, the best NHL teams can do is to send mixed messages. The NHL allowed itself to be held hostage by a small but vocal minority of players who wanted to exclude themselves from symbolic gestures of support for gay and trans fans.

In January of 2023, the Philadelphia Flyers hosted Pride Night, to show the team's support of the LGBTQ2S+ community. This wasn't unusual; by this time, most of the teams in the league had added Pride Nights to their lists of themed games. The promotion was simple: before the game, the Flyers' players would take the warm-up skate, all wearing a special jersey with the colors of the rainbow on it. Easy enough, right?

But not all the Flyers went out for warm-up. Ivan Provorov, arguably the top defenseman on the team at the time, was nowhere to be seen. Then, when it came time for the national anthem and the game to begin, Provorov was back with his teammates, wearing the famous orange Flyers' home jersey.

Word spread quickly, both in the arena and on social media. Provorov had refused to put the rainbow jersey on, had decided not to take the warm-up, but faced no discipline from the team for ignoring a club directive. After the game, he told the media that wearing rainbow colors as a show of support for the gay community went against his Russian Orthodox religion.

But the bigger question: Why would the Flyers allow Provorov to skip the skate—ignoring, essentially, what was a team rule—but allow him to play in the game? For example, what would happen if a player said he was not going to take part in an annual team visit to a children's hospital, or wouldn't wear a military-themed warm-up jersey on the night the club saluted veterans?

After the game, coach John Tortorella was asked why Provorov was allowed to play, and this was his response. "With Provy, he is being true to himself and his religion. This has to do with his belief and his religion, and it's the one thing I respect about Provy, he's always true to himself."

In 2016, when Tortorella coached Team USA at the World Cup of Hockey, he said he would bench any player who didn't stand for the national anthem. Four years later, as coach of the Columbus Blue Jackets, he said he had changed his mind—and had come to understand that protest was not an unpatriotic act. "I have learned over the years, listening and watching, that men and women who choose to kneel during this time mean no disrespect toward the flag," he said.[22]

Then, in 2021, as an ESPN analyst, he criticized Ducks forward Trevor Zegras for the "Michigan," where a player scoops the puck off the ice, lacrosse style, and then whips it into the net. It's a rare occurrence, but it's the hockey equivalent of a posterizing slam dunk. For Tortorella, the Michigan was entirely too cool, too modern, for an old-school hockey aficionado. He later apologized for that, too.

Tortorella's back and forth is representative of hockey—one step forward, one step back, apologize, take a half measure, then revert to the old school. And the Provorov/Flyers debacle opened the door for more players and teams to bail on their planned Pride commitments. Once one team—and the league itself—let an act of insubordination slide, more followed. The New York Rangers decided against having their players wear rainbow-colored jerseys in warm-ups during Pride Night.

"Our organization respects the LGBTQ+ community and we are proud to bring attention to important local community organizations as part of another great Pride Night," read a statement from the Rangers. "In keeping with our organization's core values, we support everyone's individual right to respectfully express their beliefs."

In early March of 2023, Minnesota Wild also made the last-second decision not to wear Pride-themed warm-up jerseys. The Chicago Blackhawks didn't wear Pride jerseys, citing worries over the safety of the club's Russian players. The Russians playing in North America had reason to fear retribution from Vladimir Putin—an obsessive hockey fan—and his homosexual-hating regime in their homeland.

But it wasn't just the Russians. James Reimer stole the headlines from the San Jose Sharks' Pride night when he cited his religious conviction as the reason he couldn't wear the rainbow colors. Deciding against the simple act of wearing a themed warm-up jersey is inflammatory enough in any NHL city; but to do it in the Bay Area, a place that's basically the birthplace of the gay rights movement, that just exacerbates the severity of the snub.

Reimer faced no discipline—and the Sharks published a statement from the goalie on the team's social media channels. It was a statement filled with mixed messages. Ironically, it's apropos of what Pride Nights have become in the NHL.

"For all 13 years of my NHL career, I have been a Christian—not just in title, but in how I choose to live my life daily," read the statement attributed to Reimer. "I have a personal faith in Jesus Christ, who died on the cross for my sins and, in response, asks me to love everyone and follow him. I have no hate in my heart for anyone, and I have always strived to treat everyone that [sic] I encounter with respect and kindness.

"In this specific instance, I am choosing not to endorse something that is counter to my personal convictions which are based on the Bible, the highest authority in my life.

"I strongly believe that every person has value and worth, and the LGBTQIA+, like all others, should be welcomed in all aspects of the game and hockey."

The statement was filled with so many contradictions, it needed curation. Reimer supports the idea of welcoming gay and trans people into hockey—but won't wear the jersey. He celebrates having his own convictions—even though those "personal" beliefs actually come from others (the church). If Reimer does have no hate in his heart, why would it be such an issue to make as simple a gesture as wearing a jersey for about fifteen minutes?

That's the thing about prepared statements. They strip the media of its ability to do what it's supposed to do—to poke through mounds and mounds of bullshit.

If Reimer's stance was laden with contradictions, the Staal brothers' decision not to wear Pride warm-up jerseys came with reasons that defied logic.

Eric Staal has forged a long and illustrious career in the NHL. He's played for six NHL teams, registered more than one thousand career points, and represented Canada at the Olympics. Over the course of that many seasons, a player will play in more games that he forgets than he remembers. For every hat trick game or milestone achievement, there are dozens of road trips, times that you have to play three games in four nights, and hours spent on airplanes.

Eric and his brother Marc, who played his 1,100th career game in 2022–23, decided together not to wear the special warm-up jerseys when the Florida Panthers celebrated their Pride Night. Like Reimer, they released a statement through their team.

"After many thoughts, prayers and discussions we have chosen not to wear a pride jersey tonight.

"We carry no judgment on how people choose to live their lives, and believe that all people should be welcome in all aspects of the game of hockey.

"Having said that, we feel that by us wearing a pride jersey, it goes against our Christian beliefs."

Despite the brothers asking the media not to ask any follow-up questions, the media asked follow-up questions. (As it should—no player or team should ever dictate the rules of engagement when it comes to interviews.)

And this is where it got…weird. Yes, players do forget many of the games they've played in, especially players like the Staal brothers who have each played for nearly two decades in the NHL. Yet, Eric insisted that he'd never participated in any Pride festivities at any time in his career. It didn't take long for the images to appear of Eric Staal wearing a Montreal Canadiens Pride jersey, when he played for that team in 2020–21.

Because the players choose to let their statements do the talking, the deeper questions can't be answered. If Eric wore it before, but not in 2022–23, was it the actions of other players who emboldened him and his brother?

It should be pointed out that the wide majority of NHL players supported Pride initiatives. The league's best player, Connor McDavid, said this when asked about the Edmonton Oilers' Pride Night. "I feel very strongly that hockey needs to be inclusive—and include everybody."

McDavid didn't need to say much. Really, it's just one line. But a simple statement about the need for hockey to be inclusive—that's all that was needed. It shows just how little the teams really require of their players when it comes to recognizing LGBTQ2S+ fans. Wear the rainbow jersey in warm-up. Smile. Wave. Everybody wins.

But it matters a lot when players like Provorov, Reimer, and the Staal brothers hold out—and face no consequences for doing so. Their teams, and the NHL, allowed this small group to take over the conversation. Worse, before the 2023–24 NHL season, the league announced it would not allow teams to wear themed jerseys at all. Players would not be allowed to use themed stick tape, like Pride Tape. No Pride Night rainbow jerseys, no jerseys with Indigenous art, no Diwali jerseys or Chinese New Year jerseys like the Vancouver Canucks had the previous season, no Filipino heritage jerseys like those worn by the Winnipeg Jets in 2022–23. NHL commissioner Gary Bettman said teams were still free to host themed nights and produce colorful jerseys celebrating the occasions, but they would not be allowed to wear them on the ice for warm-ups or games.

"I've suggested that it would be appropriate for clubs not to change their jerseys in warm-ups because it's become a distraction and taking away from the fact that all of our clubs in some form or another host nights in honor of various groups or causes," said Bettman. "And we rather them continue to get the appropriate attention that they deserve and not be a distraction."[23]

There's no doubt that homophobia is an issue with even those who claim to fight for racial equity. We can have discussions about race, but sexuality is an issue where the bigots can still be protected. Imagine if Provorov, the Staals, or Reimer had chosen not to wear the colors during a theme night that honored Indigenous communities or during Black History Month. The suspensions would have come quickly, and they would have been severe. But hiding behind the walls of Russian politics or of religion allows homophobia not only to exist but to be accommodated.

At least McDavid stepped up and said something, even if it was filled with caveats that we're used to seeing from NHLers who don't really stick their necks out when it comes to matters of the public interest:

"I've enjoyed all the nights in Edmonton, whether it's Pride Night or military night, Indigenous Night, all the various nights we've had and the chances to celebrate. I've always enjoyed them, I can't speak for everyone else, or the league or anything like that.

"I've expressed disappointment in not being able to wear the various jerseys, the tapes, whatever. Whether it's the Pride Tape or pink tape, or anything, it's always something I've enjoyed. In terms of a league stand-point, is it something I'd like to see put back in place someday? Certainly. But that's not the way it is right now."

In October, then Arizona Coyotes player Travis Dermott openly defied the ban, coming out for warm-up with rainbow-colored Pride Tape on his stick. With the NHL now embroiled in a PR nightmare of its own making, the Player Inclusion Coalition offered a lifeline. After consulting with the Coalition and the players' union, the ban on stick tape was reversed, and players would be able to support political and social causes individually.

It was a middle-of-the-road solution that allowed the NHL to back-pedal but not obligate teams to, well, actually support anything. The thing is, Dermott's move represented what most of the players wanted to see. A loud minority of players were allowed to hijack the Pride movement. In January of 2024, I sat in the press box, watching the Edmonton Oilers' Pride Night unfold. Reporters wore rainbow ribbons on their clothing. Television crews from both Edmonton and Seattle had rainbow tape wrapped around the bases of their microphones. During breaks in play, prominent members of Edmonton's gay community were honored on the video scoreboard. A 50–50 draw was held, with money going to the Centre for Sexual and Gender Diversity at MacEwan University.

After the game, when players were asked about Pride Night, they echoed what McDavid had said before. They weren't especially wordy, they didn't go into diatribes, but they said enough to prove that, heck, there's a large percentage of this league who don't want to be perceived as ignorant.

"Ever since I've gotten here, the city of Edmonton and this organi-zation has always been open and welcoming and inclusive," said Evander Kane. "With a night like tonight, that was no different. It was great to be a part of."

Defenseman Mattias Ekholm said: "It's great, I think this is a great thing for hockey. We want to be an inclusive environment, and I think a win like this, with the crowd, with everything going on, I think for the league and our team, it was a great night."

No one is asking players to make twenty-minute speeches. Quick statements of support went a long way, and the morning after the game, Kane and Ekholm's comments were repeated throughout my feed on X (formerly known as Twitter until 2023).

But as a whole, when it comes to homophobia, the NHL struggles to change. It's about how loud a queer-hating minority of fans and players can be, and how they are given far too much oxygen. It's easy to wonder just how much the NHL "learned" from that element within its own fan base back in 2022.

In November of that year, the NHL used its Twitter account to show support for the Team Trans–hosted All Trans Draft Tournament, which was held in Middleton, Wisconsin, which is a suburb of the state capital, Madison. This was a tournament for transgender players to celebrate the game that they loved, and around eighty skaters participated in it.

A simple tweet to show support, and a transgender team wearing jerseys with an NHL logo on them, resulted in a firestorm of social media reactions. Because the replies were so toxic, the NHL's Twitter account had to limit how people could reply to the post. If you were to look at this one tweet, and see the responses, you would likely tell the NHL's owners that changing the game's fan base is a job that's impossible.

The last word should belong to Luke Prokop, a Nashville Predators prospect who became the first person signed to an NHL contract to come out. He watched the events unfold around the banning of Pride jerseys and had this to say:

"I share the disappointment in what feels like a step back for inclusion in the NHL," Prokop posted for his social media followers. "Pride nights and Pride jerseys play an important role in promoting respect and inclusion for the LGBTQIA+ community, and it's disheartening to see some teams no longer wearing them or not embracing their significance, while the focus of others has become about the players who aren't participating rather than the meaning of the night itself.

"Everyone is entitled to their own set of beliefs but I think it's important to recognize the difference between endorsing a community and respecting individuals within it. Pride nights are an essential step towards fostering greater acceptance and understanding in hockey, and I strongly believe that, by prioritizing diversity and inclusion, we can create an environment where every player feels comfortable bringing their authentic selves to the game.

"As someone who aspires to play on an NHL team one day, I would want to enter the locker room knowing I can share all parts of my identity with my teammates."

FOUR

THE MONEY BARRIER

LOCATED IN NORTHEAST Toronto, past the point where the subway line comes to an end, the Malvern neighborhood feels like it's a world away from the Scotiabank Arena in downtown Toronto, home of the NHL's Maple Leafs.

But on this Saturday morning, an outdoor community court is filled with children and parents. A temporary ball hockey rink hosts a game, with neighborhood kids rotating in and out of the action. Stations are set up where children can test their skills, from stickhandling to passing to shooting.

This chilly early October morning is filled with the soundtrack of a hockey lover's life, the slapping of sticks, like a beautiful orchestral rhythm section or a Neil Peart drum solo. That special "thunk" that comes when a puck or an orange hockey ball smacks off the boards. There are shouts and laughter from the players on the rink.

The next day, the scene is replicated in Flemingdon Park, another Toronto neighborhood far from the luxury boxes and padded seats of an arena carrying the name of a large Canadian bank.

The City of Toronto has christened the Malvern and Flemingdon Park neighborhoods as "priority" locations. These are communities that need free outreach programs like the Hockey Diversity Alliance delivers. Families that live in these communities aren't rich. Many are new to Canada.

According to City of Toronto stats, almost half of Malvern's residents do not speak English as their first language.[1] Of the population, 21 percent live in poverty, while another 20 percent are low income. In Flemingdon Park, 70 percent of the neighborhood's first language isn't English, and the poverty rate is a near-unbelievable 35 percent.

Combine those numbers with a simple truth: hockey is expensive. A hockey stick costs hundreds of dollars. Pads and skates even more. The registration fee for the Greater Toronto Hockey League ranges between $300 and $600 per year for house league to almost $900 per year for rep leagues. Equipment, if a family can't get hand-me-downs or find discounted gear at a sports exchange, is a four-digit investment.

And ice time is pricey. It's expensive for cities to build and maintain hockey rinks, and those costs are not 100 percent covered by municipal taxes.

Take a three-and-a-half-hour flight from Toronto, northwest to Edmonton. The Alberta capital is a hockey-mad city with a metro population of around 1.5 million. For the 2023–24 season, Edmonton Minor Hockey (EMHA) is laying out $4.67 million CAD for 26,784 hours of ice rental time. There were 556 teams in EMHA at the beginning of 2023. Average out a roster of 15–20 kids per team, and that works out to about $400–$500 per player just for ice time.

And those fees don't include travel costs as well as the extra fees that every age level, organization, and team can add. There are also regular fundraisers—from bottle drives to chocolate sales. For some, the cost of hockey for a single child can exceed $10,000 per year. For many families, especially those in low-income neighborhoods, these costs are simply too much to ask.

As well, the rise of expensive academies throughout Canada and the United States, promising families to get more out of their children, to make paths easier to the NCAA or elite junior hockey, have made the game even more exclusionary.

Ken Campbell and Jim Parcels's *Selling the Dream: How Hockey Parents and Their Kids Are Paying the Price for Our National Obsession* came out in 2013, and it warned us about how the game was becoming more and more out of reach for the middle class, let alone those with even lower economic statuses. In that book, Campbell and Parcels outlined how Pro Hockey Development, a Toronto academy, charged $700 per player simply to try out for the team it sent to the annual Brick Invitational Super Novice

Hockey Tournament in Edmonton. This is the world's most prestigious tournament…for nine- and ten-year-olds. If the child gets into the tournament, then it's another $2,500 more.[2]

A decade later, and the game becomes more out of reach. Equipment and ice time have gone up. Travel costs have risen. Filling up the car with gas to take the kids to practices and games—that's shot up, too.

There are those who try to smooth out a rink that's tilting more and more in favor of the rich. To attract families in the "priority" locations, the Hockey Diversity Alliance began the 2022–23 hockey season by offering a series of events that welcomed families into the game. Kids could join in a game of ball hockey, or shoot orange balls at targets. Families could register their kids for free hockey programs. HDA founder Akim Aliu said that more than 450 kids were registered in four Toronto neighborhoods. The HDA plans to bring the program to more Toronto communities. Akim said that three NHL teams—two in Canada, one in the United States—have reached out to see if the HDA can bring their programs to their areas.

"It's a lot of lives we're touching," said Akim. "If you can't see it, it's really tough to believe it and to hope for something and to imagine for something. We [NHL players of color] came from a lot of these neighborhoods. It is a really difficult place to come out of and make it to the highest levels of hockey. A few of us were lucky enough to do that, a lot of us slipped through the cracks. And this is what this program is really tailored towards, those kids who didn't get lucky, and didn't have a family to help them with fees, and didn't have an organization that helped them with fees. We want to be that shining example to these kids, that anything is possible, no matter where you come from."

When it comes to diversifying hockey, the first—and easiest—discussion is money. Hockey is expensive to the point of being downright exclusionary. Yet, the parents and associations will talk about how much they want change, but do very little in terms of bringing change to the game. Sure, there are bursaries and PR exercises like the Jumpstart program that's administered by the retail giant Canadian Tire, but these are drops in the bucket. If hockey is to start growing again, it can't depend on the kindness of charity to bridge the constantly growing gap between what hockey costs to play and what parents can afford to pay. Charities offer Band-Aid measures; but hockey needs full-on surgery.

When hockey registration numbers dwindle and costs continue to escalate, a perfect storm of exclusion is created. For the haves, there isn't a lot of motivation to push against the tide of exclusion. That's because their kids are protected by dwindling registration numbers. Less-deserving kids make their way onto elite travel teams because the tryouts are smaller than they used to be. And parents know that money is the gatekeeper that's keeping their child on the third line of a AAA team they didn't really deserve to make. Teams travel when kids are as young as eight or nine years old. Not only do the gas, flights (sometimes), and hotels represent added costs, but they force parents to take hours and hours away from work. The truth is that it's easier to do that when you run the company, rather than if you're the employee making an hourly wage. So, when free hockey programs like the HDA's come along, there's pushback from the privileged.

While the NHL and Hockey Canada have talked about making the game more diverse—Aliu said the fledgling HDA programs got little to no support from the NHL, Hockey Canada, or local minor-hockey leagues. The issue? Throughout Canada, it's become established that putting a kid in hockey will cost a family thousands of dollars. Then along comes an organization that is offering free hockey to kids in need. Instead of being seen as an ally to hockey, as a way to bring more kids into hockey, the established hockey culture sees what the HDA is doing as a threat. And this is why Aliu believes maybe the whole system needs to be blown right up.

"We haven't been able to get anywhere, and that's a problem, because nothing we're doing is bad," he said.

"There's a reason why the NHL is 96 percent white. People of color don't feel welcome, women don't feel welcome. I honestly believe it starts at the grassroots level and bleeds all the way up.

"It's going to take a long time to restore the integrity of the game, but I think we need to start somewhere. But I think the biggest thing we need to do is hold these institutions accountable."

Matt Dumba, the Dallas Stars defenseman who belongs to the HDA, said that BIPOC players who want to create more inclusive programs for kids are swimming upstream.

"What we've been able to build in Toronto, being able to have it piloted, and getting these kids and having our own program, it wasn't easy," said Dumba. "It took a lot of work and we had a lot of sponsors. They did a great job coming together and understanding what they are really about, helping kids and trying to eradicate racism from the game. But there's so much that goes into it, when it comes to building the game and diversity. It takes years and a lot of work. It just feels like, sometimes, institutionally, it's been the same for so long that the higher-ups are unwilling to change, and they can even see change as maybe even detrimental to the foundations of the game. I believe it's the exact opposite, I think if you have more diversity, it will only grow the game, and grow the game for the better, in all aspects, the players and the fan bases."

More kids playing hockey is better for USA Hockey, Hockey Canada, and the NHL in the long term. A bigger talent pool (that is, more kids being involved in the game) means it will be harder to make rep teams. It means the rep teams will be better. It means the quality of players moving up levels will be better. It means the players who eventually make it to the NHL or other pro leagues will be better.

"The simple answer is programs like this," said Akim. "Kids don't just drop out of trees and make the NHL. It all starts from somewhere, and it's organizations like us and what we're doing, and hopefully progressing kids into the competitive stream. I honestly think it's going to take decades. It's going to take a long time to develop these kids. I hope that when we're looking 10, 20 years down the line, we are on the right side of history when it comes to promoting the game and restoring the integrity of the game.

"I do think it's going to take a long time, but I want to be part of the generation that says 'we had a lot to do with that.' I think we're on the right path to do that."

Darnell Nurse is a defenseman who regularly plays more than twenty-five minutes a night. In 2021, the Oilers rewarded him with an eight-year, $74 million USD contract extension. He's a major patron of the Free Play program.

Knowing that he was going to make Edmonton his home for a long time, Nurse began searching for charities to support. He wanted to do something that would give kids in need the opportunity to play sports. He wanted to do something that would help diversify the playing fields, courts, and rinks in Alberta's capital city.

"I've always tried to look for causes and charities to team up with that have the same values I have," said Nurse. "This is one of the first times I've seen a program, a charity and said, wow, this lines up with everything I want to be a part of. It's sport, it's very inclusive, it brings in a lot of immigrant families. My dad was an immigrant to Canada, so, that hits home for me. It gives people the chance to feel part of a community—people who may feel like outsiders in their everyday lives."

Looking back on Nurse's life, it's easy to see why the Free Play program means so much to him. He grew up in Hamilton, Ontario—a place that loves hockey (it's home to the first-ever Tim Hortons; you can find it at the corner of Ottawa Street North and Dunsmure Road) and its football. The black and gold of the Hamilton Tiger-Cats is ever present in Canada's Steel City.

That was especially true in the Nurse household. Richard Nurse, Darnell's dad, came from Trinidad and Tobago to Canada, then played football across the border at Canisius University, then spent five seasons as a wide receiver for the Ticats. But Richard wasn't the most accomplished football player in the family; Darnell's uncle, Donovan McNabb, was a bona fide NFL superstar. He was named to the Pro Bowl six times and is regarded as one of the best quarterbacks to ever wear the famous green jersey of the Philadelphia Eagles. In his career, he threw for 37,276 yards—that's more than 21 miles worth of completed passes.

Darnell's mom, Cathy, played basketball at McMaster University. His sister Kia would go on to win two American national basketball titles at the University of Connecticut and play in the WNBA. His other sister Tamika played basketball at the University of Oregon and at Bowling Green State University. And his cousin, Sarah, would go on to win the gold medal at the Beijing Winter Olympics with the Canadian national women's hockey team. She's now a star player in the Professional Women's Hockey League.

While Nurse was growing up, he also looked up to another athlete: Jarome Iginla, who spent most of his career with the Calgary Flames and would go on to score 1,300 career points and earn a spot in the Hockey Hall of Fame. For Nurse, a young hockey phenom who would make the long trek on the Queen Elizabeth Way from Hamilton to Toronto to play for the Don Mills Flyers rep program, Iginla's success in the NHL was a major inspiration. "I was a huge hockey fan because I watched Jarome Iginla," said Nurse.

In his Hall of Fame induction speech, Iginla joked that he was anything but the typical hockey kid growing up in St. Albert, an affluent Edmonton suburb. He remembered what it was like to be a minor-hockey player of color. As a kid, he looked up to other Black players who were in the NHL, or had played in the NHL and since retired. He idolized Edmonton Oiler Grant Fuhr, who had established himself as one of the best goalies in team history and grew up just west of Edmonton in the bedroom community of Spruce Grove. He knew about Willie O'Ree, and Tony McKegney, who scored 320 goals in 912 NHL games throughout the 1970s and '80s.

"Being a young, Black hockey player, it was important for me to see other Black players in the NHL," Iginla said. "In my first year of hockey, as a seven-year-old, a kid came up to me and said, 'Why are you playing hockey?' Over the years, I'd hear 'What are your chances of playing in the NHL? There's not many Black players.' I'd hear other stuff. Luckily, there were only a few. But I know it was thanks to guys like Grant and Willie who let me know that my dream of playing in the NHL was attainable."

Iginla, in turn, helped pass that dream on to a young Darnell Nurse. Ironically, Nurse would be drafted by the team that remains the Flames' bitter archrival: the Edmonton Oilers. As a young player, he was taunted.

"I definitely look back and reflect on some of those instances," said Darnell. "At the same time, I look back and see that those instances didn't change me as a person; they didn't stop me from getting to the position I'm in today. But I'm not going to say they made me stronger, because you still sit back and think about them, even today."

Nurse said it helped when white teammates and their family members spoke out against racism. "It was the best when teammates who don't look like you stick up for you—and I had that happen on multiple occasions in hockey or lacrosse," he said. "If I look back, I'm appreciative of the fact that my teammates had my back, no matter what."

Iginla said similar things after he retired. His dad came to Canada from Nigeria, and his mom hailed from Oregon in the United States. He recalled what it was like growing up, to have teammates who had his back.

"Yes, there were some incidents where something was going on in the stands…later after the game, you'd hear somebody say something inappropriate and ignorant, and one of my teammates' dads went over and talked to him," Iginla told Sportsnet.[3] "You know, those [things] meant a lot for me, to have that support from my teammates and other families. It meant a ton—it wouldn't have been the same if it's my grandpa having to go over and talk to them.

"Any racism towards anybody, it's not acceptable. And if it's parents, and you have the opportunity to [intervene] peacefully for another family, it makes a big difference," he said. "And it'll help that kid, as I'm very thankful that those parents were there for me."

After coming through the minor-hockey ranks in Metro Toronto, Nurse moved on to the Sault Ste. Marie Greyhounds, an elite junior team in the Ontario Hockey League. He was taken in the first round of the 2013 Entry Draft by the Oilers and was selected to play for Canada at the 2015 World Championships.

Free Play for Kids founder Tim Adams said that adding Nurse's support to the program, and even seeing him out there playing with the kids meant a lot. It's not super special for an athlete to endorse a charity. We see it across all major sports, across the world. What sets this deal apart is the level of engagement that Nurse has in the program. There are a lot of athletes who sign checks for hospitals or who reserve boxes at the stadiums for kids in need or for vets. But Nurse and Free Play for Kids don't have a blank-check relationship. Nurse is an active participant in the program.

"It feels like we've been fighting for a long time," said Adams. "It's nice to finally have someone like Darnell in our corner and willing to take the gloves off with us."

Kids in the Free Play program get the chance to be the "Darnell Nurse Captain of the Week" and get to go to an Oilers game.

"I couldn't even imagine going to school and to know that your parents, or whoever you came over to Canada with, they're doing everything they can to supply your everyday needs," said Nurse. "And on top of that, you're just trying to fit in. That's a lot of adjusting to do. This program gives not only an outlet to play and get support, but you see there are a lot of other people in the same position. Just looking at the charity as a whole, the program as a whole, it was kind of a no-brainer to be a part of."

Adams believes it is so important to have someone like Darnell give a "bigger megaphone" to the program because if kids of color see a Black NHL star standing up for them, it's an inspiration.

"If you don't see people like you doing the thing, that thing doesn't seem attainable," Tim said.

To get kids involved, they are bused from schools in Edmonton to a recreation center/indoor soccer center in the east side of the city. They play ball hockey, and other sports like flag football and soccer.

Why ball hockey? It's a great way to introduce kids to the game. To bring more people into hockey, we need to make ball and street hockey popular again. If you grew up in Canada, chances are your parents played a lot of street hockey and ball hockey. There would be games set up in streets, courts, driveways. For me, it offered some of my fondest childhood memories, the neighborhood kids gathered on a cul-de-sac. One net was always set up in front of my family's home, because a thick hedge surrounded the front lawn, and acted as a backstop that collected wayward shots. One of the kids that used to play street hockey in the cul-de-sac in Brampton, Ontario, was Andrew Cassels; he'd go on to play in the NHL. Years later, I was in the Columbus Blue Jackets dressing room, where he remembered me as being the "kid with the hedge." (He also remembered exploding my face with a slap shot.)

Skates and pads and composite sticks are expensive. But all you need for ball hockey is a ball, a couple of nets, and low-end sticks you can find at a sports exchange, a neighborhood sporting goods shop, a Canadian Tire, or a Dick's Sporting Goods. And, for families, street hockey and ball hockey give them the chance to try before they buy. This is especially important when a family is already working hard just to make ends meet. Registration, ice time, skates, and sticks…it's thousands of dollars. And what if hockey is not the sport for your child? That's an expensive trial process. So why not try it with a ball rather than a puck, to see if the passion is there?

Arnold Pinnock is a Canadian actor and filmmaker who created the series *The Porter*, which aired on CBC in Canada and BET+ in the United States. It was a drama set in an era when Black sleeping car porters began to organize in cities across Canada.

Pinnock, like many kids growing up in his Toronto neighborhood, discovered hockey on the street, not on the ice. "Hockey was *the* sport," he recalled. "White, yellow, green, black—it didn't matter. You taped the Sears catalogs to your shins, or whatever old pads, and you got your hockey stick and you went for it.

"My mom hated it if I put one of those orange balls through someone's car window. But she knew I was right there, playing hockey throughout the Christmas break, until the sun went down. And she knew she didn't have to worry about me. And I think every mom and every dad loves that aspect of things."

If we are going to make hockey more accessible to Canadians of varying backgrounds and income levels, we need to go back in time. We need street hockey and ball hockey to be important again, like it was before parents felt the need to put their Atom-level kids in camps run by former NHLers.

"What is the definition of hockey?" said Adams. "I don't understand why hockey is always on the ice in full equipment with two referees. But what is playing street hockey with a stick and a ball? That's hockey, too."

If we get kids playing street hockey again, it frees up rinks and introduces more kids to the game. We need to get communities to take down those signs that warn "no street hockey" is allowed.

"People always say, 'Soccer is so easy to play, all you need is a ball.' Why can't hockey be the same?" asked Adams. "Why can't it be that all you need is a stick and a ball? It doesn't have to be a fancy stick, either. You make almost anything into a ball—and, there, you're playing hockey."

By busing the kids to one central location, Free Play makes it easy for parents. Instead of having to find out about how to sign their kids up, the program comes to them. We don't often think about how hard it is to register kids for hockey, outside of the costs. A lot of times, information about where to sign up for hockey is posted at the local arenas, but really, only families already involved in hockey will see them. For parents who might only still be learning English (or French, in parts of Canada) it's not easy to find out how to register kids for sports.

"Another part is the registration piece, what it means to register, what the commitment is to register, and how to get to the arena," said Adams.

In 2022–23, the Free Play for Kids program launched the Wolves, a coed team that played in an Edmonton recreational ice hockey league. It was a low-pressure environment where kids were introduced to the game. In fact, the games were so informal, the opposing team sometimes traded players with the Wolves to make the games fairer. When the stakes aren't high, kids find a way to level the ice.

"We don't care about the outcome," said Sonny Sekhon, Free Play for Kids' chief fundraiser in 2023. "That's not what Free Play is about. We're not looking to develop the next McDavid or the next Kia Nurse. We want you to play sports so that you have a community to belong to. If you happen to be good, great."

It's a far cry from Free Play's soccer programs—where four of six teams won their respective leagues in 2023. More than any other sport that Free Play embraces, hockey is the one that requires the most effort.

"The only sport we struggle with is hockey," said Sekhon. "That's because hockey is an interesting game. If the first time you've ever been on the ice is September of this season, a win is a 7–1 loss. So, we measure our program's success differently. But every single game we had a 22-person bench. Happy kids. High-fives. Happy parents. That's because hockey's expensive, and these kids are so used to hearing that they can't afford this. And here they are, just having fun.

"It was nice to see, because I feel we taught the other teams a lot, too. They're learning that 'Hey, maybe I am privileged.'"

Nurse imagines a future when NHL dressing rooms are more diverse. "For me, the way to look at it is representation. You look at the NHL, and slowly but surely, the league is getting more diverse," he said. "But it's not at the point where you're watching hockey every night and saying 'There's someone who looks like me,' that I can see myself being one day."

Nurse's participation has led to a larger partnership between Free Play and the Edmonton Oilers, which allows for the hockey program to grow. The Edmonton Oilers Community Foundation has pledged more than $600,000 CAD to the program, annually. It's a significant sum for the program, and it's about as much as a team would spend on the contract of a fourth-line depth player. The plan moving forward is to ice more competitive teams, which meets Nurse's vision of being able to get kids of color not only onto the ice, but to the next levels of the game. Free Play takes a lot of the stressors away from kids and parents. It's not just about getting skates and sticks. It's about getting rides to the rink, when both parents are working crazy hours. It's about being able to play with kids who look like you and share similar life experiences.

"Moving forward, with a bigger partnership with the Oilers, we want to lean into changing the way the game is played," said Sekhon. If you're five, six, or seven years old, why shouldn't you be able to play? If you came here as a refugee, why should you not be able to play Canada's game? What I love about the Free Play model is that you're not applying for a grant that you don't understand. You're not trying to find equipment. You just come to Free Play and, when we have enough players, we will put you in the league. You don't have to worry about getting a ride to the game, getting the equipment, or paying the fees. And you're on a team with a lot of people in the same situation."

As much as we think that it's just great to get more children onto the ice, once kids fall in love with the game, there needs to be a clear path for them to move forward; it can't be "Well, it's great you're standing out in this community league, but to move forward you'll need to join a league that's going to cost your parents thousands and thousands of dollars they don't have." It will take a village, but it's time to end the culture of hockey as being suburban parents driving kids to practices in $75,000 SUVs.

Programs like the HDA's inner-city free hockey initiative and Free Play for Kids are just starting points for the game. The danger is that they merely become showcase programs that exist to make everyone feel better about themselves, like how putting your recycling out in the blue box makes you feel you're fighting climate change. The danger is that these programs remain on the fringes, that these players get the worst possible ice times and don't get the chance to integrate into the hockey-league structure. It's so easy for the powers that be to see the kids of color, the underprivileged, skating around for an hour each Sunday morning, as the sun is rising, and think that's good enough. That progress has been made.

Nurse said it is important that programs that make hockey more accessible cannot just be about giving at-risk kids an hour at the rink a week. We need to give these kids great coaching and find ways to get the kids who are special a path toward rep teams.

"A big part of it is representation, and that's not only the grassroots part of the game, but also giving some of the better talent who are diverse the same opportunities when they're coming up," he said. "When they're 13, 14, 15, 16 years old, getting the skills trainers and the coaching so they can have the same opportunities to get to the next level. That's where my mind goes. Having those kids have access to those types of resources, to be able to push to the next level, will make the league more diverse."

To really tackle the exclusionary costs of hockey, we need to ask some hard questions about what have become accepted practices—from placing kids under the age of ten on travel teams, to putting composite sticks that cost hundreds of dollars each in their hand.

In June of 2023—in minor hockey's off-season—I searched the Dick's Sporting Goods website for deals on ice hockey sticks. From the major brands like Bauer and CCM, the prices ranged $160–$350 per stick. In Canada, Sport Chek had clearance sticks for as low as $110 CAD, but for top-end sticks, it's about $400.

Do kids need expensive composite sticks? The answer is no. Actually, hell no. This comes straight from Minnesota Hockey's guide on how to choose the right stick for your kids. The basic, old-fashioned (and cheaper) wood stick is just fine for your eight-year-old. The guide spells it out: "Many coaches still recommend using wood sticks at the younger age groups because of the advantages they provide for puck handling and catching passes," and "in most cases, you get what you pay for as the higher prices usually indicate a higher the quality of materials and better performance, but top-of-the-line sticks aren't really necessary for youth hockey players."[4]

So why won't minor-hockey associations step in and ban composite sticks for kids, which would be at least a small step toward driving down costs and making the game more equitable? In Alberta, teen baseball players have to stop using aluminum and "showcase" bats by the time they get to the U15 level. They can only use wood and wood-composite bats. Sure, wood bats break—but most kids aren't seeing 98 mph fastballs that come in on the hands. Seeing a bat break at that level is rare. My son is in his third year of using a wood bat, and he's broken just one, and that was off a pitching machine, not game play.

Why don't the leaders of grassroots hockey organizations do the same? It's the power of the sports-equipment industry, which tells us you need to spend more, to get the latest gear, that sports science actually matters to a kid who learned how to skate the previous winter.

And we need to ask, who is benefiting from this? The kids, or the SUV-driving white suburban parents who get to bask in the glow of watching their kids play on rep teams, and get to wear the cool sweatshirts and jackets?

"You can't pay your way into the NHL—it's always going to be a lottery," wrote Campbell and Parcels. "But the thing is, the lottery tickets get more expensive all the time. That means only the privileged kids get their names in the hat."[5]

Karl Subban, the father of pro hockey players P. K, Malcolm, and Jordan, was a child when his family moved from Jamaica to Canada. It was in the northern mining city of Sudbury where Karl fell in love with hockey and became a fan of the most dominant team of the era—the Montreal Canadiens. For Karl, though, being part of a hardworking immigrant family, who had to count every nickel, meant that playing organized hockey was never going to happen for him.

"On one hand, I had a growing passion for the game," Subban wrote in *How We Did It: The Subban Plan for Success in Hockey, School and Life.* "On the other hand, I was having difficulty accepting the fact that I couldn't play hockey on a real team since my family could not afford the equipment, the registration fees and the travel. I had this burning desire to play more and achieve more, but my dream of being Ken Dryden had almost no shelf life."[6]

Every year, the West Edmonton Mall hosts the Brick Invitational Hockey Tournament. This tourney brings together some of the top novice-age players from across North America. The 2023 tournament had teams from Minnesota, Connecticut, Michigan, Illinois, Pennsylvania, Saskatchewan, Manitoba, Quebec, Ontario, and, of course, Alberta. Teams carry names like "Toronto Pro Hockey," "Connecticut Jr. Rangers," and "Montreal Canadiens" to give them an air of professionality.

I mentioned these were novice-age players, right? These are kids who are years away from puberty, and they're being shuffled on road trips. Parents burn their vacation time so they can go to Edmonton. Sorry, no Disneyland this year, kids. Beaches are so overrated (though the West Edmonton Mall does have an indoor water park that locals refer to as "20-dollar-Mexico").

The rep-sports, travel-team complex is something that perplexes the European players who come to the NHL. Victor Hedman, the Swedish star defenseman for the Tampa Bay Lightning, wrote about how in his home country, "rep" and "travel" teams don't happen till the teenage years. Kids play hockey in their hometowns. For fun. It's accessible and the pressure is off.

"I hear stories about youth hockey in America and Canada, and kids jumping around from team to team. There's all kinds of travel teams you have to try out for, and expensive camps, and coaches to impress," Hedman wrote in *The Players' Tribune*.[7] "But in Sweden, it's more of a family atmosphere. At least when I was young. I know it has changed a bit lately. Until I was 14, there were no 'tryouts.' If you're born in O-vik [Örnsköldsvik], you play for MoDo or one of the other local teams. In fact, the Sedin twins and Markus Naslund played for a team called Järved, on an outdoor rink. There are different levels, but you are never cut. When people talk about Swedish hockey, they often mention the 'chemistry' of the players. But really, it's a total philosophy of community that starts when you're young."

About twenty years ago, I wrote a feature about the Swedish city of Örnsköldsvik, a forestry hub of a little more than thirty thousand residents. At the time, it was the hottest of hockey hotbeds—producing then superstars like Markus Naslund, Peter Forsberg, and the Sedin twins, who were all near the top of the NHL's scoring charts.

"We have a good program there for players when they reach the age where you would finish high school—about 16 to 17 years old," said Naslund. "That's the age when you can really develop as a hockey player. We had a lot of good guys when I was there and that created a lot of good competition between us."[8]

Note that Naslund gave the prime development years as coming in the late teens—not at novice age. He also spoke about how important it was to keep a group of friends together and not break them up into travel teams, the haves and have-nots, at an early age.

As of the writing of this book, there were 106 Swedes in the NHL, from a country that has 10.5 million people. Imagine that New York City produced 106 NHLers. You can't. Yet, the population of NYC and Sweden are comparable.

So, maybe, just maybe, our exclusionary, cost-heavy North American system, with the summer hockey and the dryland training and the hotel stays and the camps run by someone who played half a season in the NHL as a fourth liner, are just...

Bullshit.

But this drive to send kids away to academies, to spend tens of thousands a year, to put a metaphorical "do not enter" sign on arenas for those who are poor or outside the suburban SUV-mom class, where did it begin?

Really, it's all part of the mythology we've built around the game, and what it takes to succeed. I may get my Canadian passport taken away for writing this, but some of this begins with the story of Wayne and Walter Gretzky.

In Canada, the story of Wayne Gretzky's upbringing is almost biblical in the way it is passed down from generation to generation. The famous backyard rink in Brantford, Ontario. Wayne and his father, Walter, spending their Saturday nights watching *Hockey Night in Canada*, with the son dutifully drawing up diagrams of where the players skated on the ice. It has become the blueprint for hockey parents, an example of the perfect relationship between parent and child.

As hard as it might be, we need to accept that it's not a universal story. A backyard rink is something most kids are never going to have. No one should take for granted the ability for a father to devote that much time to his son's hockey career. We have to see the privilege within the Gretzky story even though, for decades, we have chosen not to. There are families who work multiple jobs and don't even have time to take their kids to one Saturday or Sunday game a week let alone four or five practices per week.

In 1998, Dan Bylsma and his father, Jay, coauthored *So Your Son Wants to Play in the NHL?* Using their own tale of perseverance, they meant the book to be an oracle for hockey parents who wanted their kids to realize their dreams (or, to realize their parents' dreams).

Dan Bylsma played 429 NHL games in Los Angeles and Anaheim and, eleven years after the book was published, coached the Pittsburgh Penguins to a Stanley Cup championship. There's no doubt that the Bylsma method worked, but it's a method that requires a lot of capital—the kind of wherewithal most of us don't have. Jay wrote about taking time off from his work as an investment banker to focus on his kids and their sports careers. And, yes, a backyard rink (and also a golf hole) was a key ingredient in encouraging his sons' sports development.

"I'm not sure if there was any correlation in the fact that the sons of the fathers who were most involved got the scholarships, but I'd like to think there was," he wrote.[9]

But the messages of privilege are so blatant. Hockey is not meant for working-class parents. It's not for the inner cities of North America. The sacrifice of time is available to only those who can afford it. Success is reserved for the obsessive, and those who can pull out all the stops for their kids.

This is not meant to disparage the accomplishment of "making it" as a professional athlete. Getting to any major pro league, even for a player who gets called up for one solitary game at the elite level, is the result of thousands of hours of hard work and sacrifice. It is a major personal accomplishment.

Bylsma's assertion that the kids who get scholarships are the ones whose fathers are there for them more often and not is a powerful one. Even though it was made two decades ago, it still plays to the hockey stereotype, that parents have to sacrifice weekends, vacation time, and tens of thousands of dollars to ensure their hockey-playing kids get the ice time they need.

A NARRATIVE OF RICH, WHITE FAMILIES

A little more than a decade ago, I flew to southern California to write a profile of the Comrie family.

At the time, Eric Comrie was a true NHL prospect and a member of the Tri-City Americans, a major junior team based in Kennewick, Washington, that played in the Western Hockey League. His older brothers, Paul and Mike, had already played in the NHL. Paul's career was all too brief, cut short by a major head injury. He played just 15 games for the Edmonton Oilers. Mike played 11 seasons in the NHL, until hip problems forced him out of the game.

Their father, Bill, showed me around the family mansion in Newport Coast, which acted as a home away from home for one of Canada's wealthiest men. The stunning views of the Pacific Ocean. The manicured golf hole that took up a chunk of the backyard. The full-size outdoor rink, with a surface that could be flooded and frozen even in the heat of a California afternoon.

When I asked Bill when I could speak to Eric, he said I just needed to wait for him to finish his session with Andy O'Brien, one of the most in-demand personal trainers in North America. O'Brien had worked with top NHL stars and Olympians such as Patrick Chan, owner of three figure skating medals, including one gold.

Raised in Edmonton, Bill was a top hockey prospect and was offered a shot to make the Chicago Black Hawks roster. But in 1971, after the sudden passing of his father, he took over the family's furniture business and renamed it The Brick. By offering store credit and layaway plans—now common in the world of big-ticket sales—Comrie transformed the small family furniture business into one of the largest retail empires in Canada. By 2023, there were 220 Brick stores across Canada. And, yes, it's the same Brick that sponsors that massive novice invitational tournament held every year in Edmonton.

Years after my profile of the Comrie family was published, Eric would go on to make the NHL; he's played for the Winnipeg Jets, Detroit Red Wings, New Jersey Devils, and Buffalo Sabres.

Bill maintained that his kids were never shielded from the hard work it took to succeed in life. The boys who made it in the NHL went to regular high schools; they rode the buses with their teammates; they learned to live away from home.

"Dad always taught us the value of money, and that you have to work very hard in order to get success," said Eric. "We know his success was based on hard work, and it's something that influences me every single day."

No matter the hard work, it's clear that the Comries also benefited from the privilege of being born into wealth. In the NHL, their story isn't really all that rare. There are other NHLers whose multimillion-dollar contracts actually represent pay cuts from what they could have made if they just would have stayed in the family business. Zach Hyman, who has starred for the Toronto Maple Leafs and Edmonton Oilers, is the son of multimillionaire Stuart Hyman, who famously bought scores of junior teams in Ontario and added a scouting service to his portfolio when Zach was draft age.

Joe Colborne played 295 NHL games with the Maple Leafs, Calgary Flames, and Colorado Avalanche. His dad, Paul, founded Star Valley Oil and Gas and has been at the head of more than a dozen companies in the oil and gas industry.

Of course, there are many kids of former NHL players who are currently excelling in the game. There are the Tkachuk brothers—Brady and Matthew—who star for the Ottawa Senators and Florida Panthers, respectively, as of this writing. There's Toronto Maple Leafs superstar William Nylander. Tage Thompson is the Buffalo Sabres' top forward, and he's an NHL son. Paul Stastny's dad is in the Hockey Hall of Fame. Calgary Flames defenseman Tyson Barrie's dad skated in the NHL. Vancouver Canucks forward Jake DeBrusk and Philadelphia Flyers forward Sean Couturier have NHL lineage. That's also true for Jakob Chychrun, a star defenseman who plays for the Washington Capitals. Colorado Avalanche defenseman Josh Manson. Sam Gagner, who has had three stints over a long NHL career. The three Hughes brothers are rising stars in the NHL and in the American hockey program, but they grew up in Toronto, where their ex-player dad worked for the Maple Leafs. There's Marcus and Nick Foligno, and veteran forward Max Domi.

You could stock an entire team's roster with the kids of NHLers, which shows just how helpful it is to be born into a professional hockey culture, where a hockey arena is where Dad goes to work.

Yes, it's easy for me to cherry-pick examples of rich kids who made it to the NHL. But try to find the poor-kid-who-made-it narratives in hockey like you do in other major team sports. It's tough. Soccer's legends—Pele, Lionel Messi, Diego Maradona—they all inspired a planet with how they rose from the poorest slums in South America to greatness. Basketball is filled with stories of kids, both from the United States and around the world, who escaped poverty by perfecting their talents in high school gyms, playgrounds, and community centers. While baseball's North American players are part of a growing pay-to-play, academy system, the game has been changed by the influx of players from the Dominican Republic and Venezuela who learned to play with makeshift gloves and cracked bats.

Their talent won out above all. In hockey, the "poor" kids come from the middle class, whose parents overextended themselves to pay the tens of thousands of dollars per year it takes to put their kids through elite hockey.

In Canada, the hockey rink is mythologized as a community gathering place, where parents sit on cold benches, swapping stories while sucking back double-doubles from Tim Hortons. In truth, the hockey rink is one of the most bougie places you can find. Its parking lot is filled with climate-killing extended pickups and luxury SUVs with automated lift gates. Kids who still need to have their gloves taped to sticks in order to learn how to grip them properly are wearing thousands of dollars' worth of gear. The coffee isn't from Tim Hortons; the travel mugs are the bedazzled Starbucks variety. The rink is a place that screams wealth and privilege.

The money barrier is the first topic of discussion when it comes to opening up the game. The thing is, privilege is wound into the lore of minor hockey—to the point where we can't see what's right in front of us. Even those of us trying to break through some of the larger social issues in hockey have a hard time finding a way around the financial barriers that exist in the game.

Case in point: In 2023, in a major event held right outside the front doors of Rogers Place, the Edmonton Female Hockey Alliance was launched. It's a major undertaking—a league aimed at bringing together the nearly 1,300 girls playing minor hockey in one of the world's true hotbeds for the sport. During the ceremony, founding committee member Aimee Skye said the league would have an "unwavering commitment to an excellent player experience." This is a league where girls came first and do not have to be the square pegs in hockey organizations that set up their programs with boys' needs in mind.

But Skye admitted that the league would cost families more than where the girls previously played. "A lot of that is really a commitment to saying 'we're building a fantastic experience for players,'" she said. "And, sometimes, fantastic experiences require more investment and more costs."

Included in those costs was a $200 CAD development fee.

Hockey is a sport that demands large financial commitments, and even larger commitments when it comes to time. The equipment alone costs thousands of dollars and needs regular replacement. Kids grow. Hockey skates can cost four digits. Composite sticks that cost hundreds of dollars are a far cry from the $50 wood sticks we could get at the sporting goods store a generation ago.

The elite teams travel, and that's especially onerous on American families, since top-level teams can't be found in every state, let alone in every city. If you don't grow up in New England, Michigan, or Minnesota, you might still be able to find hockey programs, but high-level teams might be scarce.

Jason Zucker was the first player ever drafted who hailed from the state of Nevada. To get to that elite level, his parents sent him to California to play minor hockey there. They flew him out from Vegas to Los Angeles regularly.

In a lot of the material I've read on the rising costs of hockey, the message is the same. The costs are institutionalized, it needs to change, but you can't blame well-heeled parents for passing on their privilege to their kids. What parent doesn't want to do whatever they can to help their kid succeed?

I'll disagree. I think we all need to look at the shrinking registration numbers, the TV ratings that aren't nearly what they once were, and recognize the money pit is slowly killing the game. Hockey is in danger of becoming polo, a sport seen as played only for elites by elites.

Adidas's seven-year deal to produce jerseys for the NHL teams expired when the commissioner presented the Stanley Cup to the team that won the 2024 championship. The German apparel giant chose not to renew. The short-term gains of selling $300 sticks to ten-year-olds is being replaced by long-term losses—and sports giants just don't see hockey as big enough, strong enough, for their marketing dollars.

Cost is a major reason hockey remains as white as it does. It's definitely not the only one. Hockey and sociology expert Courtney Szto (see earlier chapter) called the issue of cost a low-hanging fruit when it comes to discussing what needs to change in the sport.

"The pillar of access is the most comfortable pillar for folks, because it doesn't overtly ask people to reckon with race, when they can instead reckon with class," she said in her keynote address at the online Growing the Game Summit.[10]

"Just know that when you give a child a hockey bag full of gear, that you have just invited them into a space based on racial segregation and colonization. There must be equal work that goes on to addressing those histories, as well."

And that's why the issue of cost is dealt with at this point in this book. There are other discussions that need to be had, many of them far more uncomfortable than the price of ice time, sticks, and goalie pads.

FIVE

YOU MADE IT, NOW FOLLOW THE STEREOTYPE, PLEASE

T HE DATE: JANUARY 29th, 1997, in the midst of Anson Carter's rookie NHL season as a member of the Washington Capitals. Carter was in an up-and-down campaign. That's not unusual for any NHL rookie; it's a big jump to play in the world's best league, even for a player who was ripping up the NCAA the previous season. Up to that point, Carter had played most of his games with the Capitals' minor-league affiliate in Portland, Maine.

But after that night's game with the Philadelphia Flyers, Carter was contacted by Barry Trotz, the coach of the Portland Pirates. As Carter recalls, Trotz proudly told the young player that he was in the NHL to stay. There would be no more trips to the minors.

Was it because Carter had scored a key goal, or had racked up a couple of assists? After all, he averaged better than a point a game during his collegiate career at Michigan State University. In 1995, he was a finalist for the Hobey Baker Award, which goes to the top male hockey player in the NCAA.

No, he hadn't scored in that game against the Flyers. He didn't set up a goal, either. In fact, the Caps had lost the game by a 2–1 count. What Carter had done was fight. He scrapped with Flyers forward Rod Brind'Amour in the second period.

"I ran [Flyers defenseman] Eric Desjardins behind the net, we were playing Philadelphia, I beat up Rod Brind'Amour, my first fight in the league, and Trotzy called me after and said, 'See you later kid, I don't expect to see you back down here in the AHL,'" recalled Carter. "That's when the light went on for me. It's clear that these guys want to make me into a tough guy—but that wasn't going to happen."

At the start of his rookie season, Carter was placed on the fourth line with two scrappers. Despite his scoring pedigree in the NCAA, he was never placed on the first or second lines, even for a look-see. He was eventually dispatched to the minors, where he had an impressive 38 points in 27 games. So, he came back up—and was expected to fight, again.

"I started the season on the fourth line with Craig Berube and Kevin Kaminski. I had an assist in my second game, and then I got sent down because I wasn't creating enough offense," Carter recalled.

"I go down to Barry Trotz's team—the best coach in the AHL, obviously; he won an AHL Championship a couple of years before that. First line, I think I had 19 goals in 27 games in the AHL. [19 goals and 19 assists, actually.] It was something crazy. We were the best team [in the AHL] by far back then. And I get called up, and I'm on the fourth line again. And I'd watch all these young players, [Jaroslav] Svejkovsky, Andrew Brunette, and all these guys would get the chance to play on the top line with Michal Pivonka and Peter Bondra, and I'm on the fourth line. And I get sent down again.

"I looked at myself and said what the hell is going on, why am I not playing on the top line, or in the top six players? I'm a leading scorer in the AHL, why am I not playing with better players?"

His first season in the NHL flew against the brave predictions of then Capitals general manager David Poile. "Anson was one of the best players in the country as a junior [in college] and he should be an NHL player one day," Poile told the *Washington Post* in 1996.[1] "He's a hard-driving power forward who's at his best when he plays with high intensity. He's going to score some goals just by getting to the net with the puck more often."

What set Carter apart from Svejkovsky or Brunette was the color of his skin. Carter believes he was the victim of racial stereotyping. Growing up in the Toronto area, the son of Barbadian immigrants, Carter didn't see a lot of Black hockey players on TV. When he did, they were fighters—guys like Val James, the first US-born Black player to make it to the NHL, who spent time with the Buffalo Sabres and Toronto Maple Leafs as an enforcer. There was Bill Riley, who had 320 penalty minutes in 139 career games with the Washington Capitals and Winnipeg Jets.

In the 1990s, Peter Worrell, Georges Laraque, and Donald Brashear were all top-level heavyweight enforcers in the league. Yet, Carter desperately wanted to prove that a Black pro hockey player didn't have to "make it" through his fists—he wanted to show people that a Black player could make it to the NHL by the way he skated, passed, and shot.

At the trade deadline, the Caps sent Carter to the Boston Bruins.

The fighter is a role that has been downplayed in hockey in recent years. Most teams in the modern NHL don't carry guys on the roster who only play three or four minutes a night and are really only out there to drop the gloves. A generation ago, every team, from junior hockey to the minors to the NHL, had at least one enforcer on their rosters. Many teams had entire fourth lines made up of scrappers. They were loved by fans but had arguably the toughest job of all. General managers and coaches believed that teams needed a "policeman" to respond to any displays of intimidation from the other team. If a star player took a questionable hit, the fighter would be sent out to settle the score. If a coach felt his team had lost momentum, he'd tap his enforcer on the shoulder, asking him to fight the other team's tough guy in order to change the feel of the game. It was the show within the game—mythologized in movies like *Slap Shot* and *Youngblood*.

And it was the easiest way for players of color to be accepted into the game.

During the 1989–90 season, Robin Bawa, the first player of South Asian descent to crack the NHL, racked up seasons in the minors where he got close to 400 penalty minutes—a whopping number. He played in 61 games with the Washington Capitals, Vancouver Canucks, Mighty Ducks of Anaheim, and the San Jose Sharks, but he spent nearly a decade dropping the gloves in minor-league stops like Kalamazoo, Milwaukee, Baltimore, and Fort Wayne.

From Stan Jonathan to Chris Simon to Gino Odjick to Carter's former teammate, Berube, fans from the 1970s to the 1990s saw that the route for Indigenous players to make it in the NHL would be as tough guys. Odjick passed away from a rare heart ailment in 2023, and, tragically, Simon took his own life in 2024, with his family blaming CTE as the root cause.

Yes, it would be wrong of me not to mention some exceptions. Reggie Leach, a Stanley Cup–winning sniper with the Philadelphia Flyers, and Bryan Trottier, a Hockey Hall of Famer who was part of the New York Islanders' four-championship dynasty, broke the mold of the Indigenous-player-as-fighter; and Tony McKegney was the first Black player to score thirty goals in an NHL season. He did it four times in his career. The influence of these players can't be understated, but we also know they were vastly outnumbered by BIPOC players who got to the NHL by playing the tough-guy card.

It's not hard to figure out how the game could create so many angry men of color. Laraque was regularly called the n-word as he rose through the ranks of Quebec minor hockey; the racial abuse was so bad, his parents quit watching him play. They couldn't stand it.

James channeled his response to racist epithets through his fists. "When the racist insults came from the mouth of an opponent, I had a ready response: I would crack the guy's skull," he wrote in his autobiography.[2]

In his memoir, *Call Me Indian*, Fred Sasakamoose looked back on his time playing elite junior hockey for the Moose Jaw Canucks, on his path to becoming a Chicago Black Hawk. In this small Saskatchewan city, he and teammate Ray Leacock became fast friends; Sasakamoose, as an Indigenous man, identified with Leacock, who was Black. They were both outsiders. He remembered that during a road game in Lethbridge, Alberta, back in 1951, the fans pelted Leacock with lumps of coal, which ignited a brawl. The police had to be called in to settle things down.[3]

Willie O'Ree had fans attack him in a penalty box; James saw fans holding hand-drawn caricatures of him wearing a grass skirt, holding a spear. They heard racial slurs on the ice, as opposing players—and more importantly, their coaches—saw it as fair game to get under their skin. Is it any wonder that the very few players of color coming up through the ranks dropped the mitts frequently? How could anyone be asked to hold in that kind of anger?

And for the teams on which they played, why stop a system that—through its very whiteness—was churning out fearsome tough guys? After all, the old hockey school had established that fighting sells tickets. In the

1970s, the game had gotten to the point where the sideshow of fighting was arguably the calling card of the game, not slick passes, great saves, or booming slapshots. It was the Broad Street Bullies and *Slap Shot*. While fighting's importance has receded through the years, it's still there.

While the '70s and early '80s represented the height of fighting in hockey, the stereotypes about Black and Indigenous players were strongly established before the color lines in hockey, or even baseball, had been broken. As noted in his autobiography, *A Fly in a Pail of Milk*, the late Herb Carnegie asked former pro hockey and football player Red Storey for his recollections of playing against the author. It was Storey who claimed that Toronto Maple Leafs owner Conn Smythe had said "I will give $10,000 to anyone who can turn Carnegie white." (Carnegie himself never spoke to Smythe in his life, but recalls being watched by the famed team owner when he played junior hockey in Toronto.) Storey also wrote about his surprise when he saw Carnegie for the first time, because his mindset in the 1930s was that Black kids just didn't play hockey.

"The guy was so good, I just couldn't believe it," wrote Storey. "First of all, Black athletes were boxers, they were football players, but no one played hockey."[4] That stereotype, of the player of color as a fighter, of being out of place in hockey, carried forth. Even three decades after O'Ree skated in his first NHL game, chances are not only that a Black player would be expected to fight, but that it would be his job description.

P. K. Subban was a top minor-hockey prospect in the Toronto area in the early 2000s, nearly a decade after Carter broke into the NHL. And that stereotype still existed. He was a smooth skating prospect, a defenseman who modeled his game after some of the best blue-line playmakers the game had ever seen, like Paul Coffey and Bobby Orr. He was a kid with jaw-dropping talent and a penchant for tape-to-tape passes.

He recalled that when he played in the OHL Cup, an Ontario showcase event for the top U16 AAA teams in the province, he was asked to do something he didn't want to do. He said that a coach on the Markham Islanders bench asked Subban to slash an opposing player across the back of the legs, as soon as the puck was dropped for the opening face-off. Subban followed his coach's orders, and got tossed out of the game for it.

"Once I got to age 15 or 16, it was always about going over the top," said Subban. "My dad [Karl] didn't like that. He didn't like me focusing on that area of the game, and not focusing on what I was there to do, working on my game to make it to the NHL. I'll never forget this, I slashed a player on the back of the leg, and the player went down. At that point, I had gotten a five-minute penalty, kicked out of the game. After the game, my dad says to me, 'P. K., you're in the OHL Cup, this is the biggest stage for you in your career, and you're out of the game because you're doing something that the coach has told you to do.' But I was like, 'But Dad, what do you want me to do? The coach is telling me to set the tone.' And my dad told me, 'I don't care, you don't slash anybody like that.'"

And Subban said that whenever he rose to a new level in the game, he had to deal with coaches who didn't believe he could succeed as a skill player—that he had to dumb down his game. "It seemed like a trend when I got to the higher levels of the game where it was the coaches, oftentimes, who would say, 'Yeah you've got skill, but you're probably not going to be a 60-point defenseman in the National Hockey League, you're probably going to be a 30-point defenseman and you'll stay in the game because of your ability to play both ways.' And I was like, there's a lot of things I can do on the ice that not a lot of other guys can do. How can they not see that?"

When Subban was selected by the Montreal Canadiens in the second round of the 2007 draft, he was six years away from winning the Norris Trophy as the NHL's best defenseman. There was no doubt that he was an exciting prospect, the kind of player who could be the cornerstone of a franchise trying to rediscover its past glory. The Canadiens aren't so much a team as they are a religion, the most decorated team in hockey, the famous bleu, rouge, et blanc jerseys that haven't changed since the likes of Howie Morenz and Elmer Lach were posing with the Stanley Cup. The spotlight that shines on a player in Montreal is just that little bit more intense than anywhere else; added into the mix are French Canadian nationalism and the knowledge that Quebec is very much a cultural enclave within North America. You cannot be *only* a hockey player in Montreal; when you don the jersey, you become an ambassador and carry the weight of history. The famed line "To you from failing hands we throw the torch be yours to hold it high," from John McCrae's famous First World War poem, "In Flanders Fields," is famously displayed in the Habs' dressing room. But the truth is, many players have been burned by the torch. The media pressure, the expectation, it can be a cross that's just too heavy to bear. The pressure was something Subban felt from day one.

"In Montreal, everyone was trying to rein me in and have me play this certain style of game," Subban said. "But this isn't me. This isn't who I am. I definitely feel like, structurally and institutionally, I was marginalized because of the expectation. The expectation wasn't for me to be a player who can play the game like a Bobby Orr, skate with the puck or have that type of impact.

"And if they did know that, they wanted to manage that. That's the way it felt like. I was never put in a position to be seen as one of the greatest defenseman to play."

Even though Subban pledged to raise $10 million for a children's hospital in Montreal, he felt that he could never escape the criticism, or at least be judged by the same parameters as elite white defensemen.

"For me, I just didn't understand it. I'm doing so many good things, on and off the ice. I'm not partying in clubs and getting in trouble. I keep my nose clean. I work with my charity, everything is productive. Why do I get these personal attacks on my character? Why is everything about me being selfish, when all I do is give? I've got more assists than goals. I've donated more money than any other player in the league. I've given my time, I've always been a likable guy, so where is this coming from? I think it's jealousy and the culture. You have to remember, there's a lot of executives who have never played or worked with a person who looks like me before. I think there's a lot of people who went to school with no one who looked like me. I think it was a big adjustment for someone to come in and play for the Montreal Canadiens and be that skilled, that talented, to be that confident, to speak differently, to dress differently than most people did at that time. When I came into the NHL, there were so many things that were coming all at once. I didn't like the fact that I had to succumb to that kind of commentary.

"It's all those things and it comes in different wrapping paper, in different packages. But it was definitely something I noticed in my career—and I had to deal with it. But I choose not to make excuses, I just try to help the game so there are more guys who look like me who don't have to go through that stuff."

Racial stereotypes are powerful, and last generations. It's something that Kim Davis, the NHL's vice president who works to make the game more diverse and inclusive, sees when it comes to how she's viewed in Manhattan boardrooms. She understands that example can be applied to how players of color are seen on the ice.

"The whole notion of bias, conscious or otherwise, usually is rooted in lack of exposure and lack of awareness," says Davis. "Coupled with lack of exposure and lack of awareness is this notion of myths that people have created for certain groups.

"When I was in corporate America, there was always this idea that Black women were angry. There was this whole myth around the angry Black woman, when we were beginning to have these uncomfortable conversations about why Black women weren't making more progress, particularly on Wall Street. Especially a few years ago, when I was in financial services, this myth would come up. So, I started talking about how we have to become myth-busters. Where does it come from? Is it media-driven? Is that someone's experience with one person? These kinds of myths get created, for the most part, around underrepresented and under-indexed audiences. The linchpin there is that often people don't have exposure to them, so these myths and fantasies get made up."

Mark Fraser provides an example of how racial issues bleed into hockey's culture—and how a player has to be forced to accept that he's not going to change things. Instead of fighting against the culture, Fraser learned how to survive within the culture.

Fraser grew up in the Ottawa area, and he knew one thing: not only would he have to play well, but he'd also have to reinvent himself. He wasn't entirely himself at the rink. Every day, he'd go in and act in a way he thought the adults running the program would want to see. He cut his hair short. He made sure not to dress differently than his teammates when they went to and from the rink.

He wasn't exactly living a lie, but he certainly wasn't being himself, either.

"You're encouraged not to be yourself," said Fraser. "A lot of times in the spaces as a racialized hockey player, sometimes it's just your appearance. It's how you're dressed.

"My ears are pierced. I currently have dreadlocks. These are things I would not have dared to do going into a locker room when I was playing. There were a number of reasons, but more than anything, it was encouraged not to do that. It was encouraged because it wouldn't be familiar to the palate of whoever was making the decisions on my career."

So, as a player coming through the ranks in Ontario, Fraser lived a double life. Mark at the arena wasn't the same as Mark away from the arena. "I would say that some of the barriers I faced were that, knowing for me to exist, I would have had to alter myself every day, to be more familiar to the environment I was going into," Mark said. "It wasn't something I would have had to do to go to school, it was not something I would have to do to go to the mall, to go shopping, or to a concert or to church. But, to go into the arena, almost every time I would have to make sure I was fitting into a 'proper' demographic and version of myself. Something that would land well in that space, something that would be familiar, that would be accepted, something that would be cohesive. I'd try not to be too different."

Fraser did excel, and he made it to the NHL. He played 219 career games with the New Jersey Devils, Toronto Maple Leafs, and Edmonton Oilers, and is now working for the Leafs in player development, focusing on equity, diversity, and inclusion.

Fraser said that, "for the most part," his minor-hockey teammates were very accepting of him, but there were occasional incidents and microaggressions. What's amazing is how often, throughout my research for this book, athletes of color looked for ways to be conciliatory and forgiving. The "there was some racism here and there, but it was something I got used to" lines show just how cautious players are when it comes to being seen as angry.

"From a general perspective, my teammates were always very accepting," said Mark. "But kids do say stupid things and gestures were definitely made, comments and jokes, too. And it gets under your skin, sometimes. But what are you going to do? While you may not already be in tune with the different layers of your identity, you're very well aware that you are different. You're well aware that you look different. And there were often reminders from teammates, even if it was a tease or a joke."

Courtney Szto writes that players of color are often forced to lead double lives at the rink. They need to fight for their place on the team, or even in the stands—but, once they "make it," they need to blend in with the white norm. "When it comes to hockey, racialized Canadians are often to (repeatedly) create a space for themselves, whereas most white Canadian men, and increasingly white women (or those able to pass as white), have symbolic space reserved for them." She later writes that "self-policing results from being concurrently invisible and hypervisible."[5]

As a white journalist, for decades I paid no mind to the sacrifices that players of color would have to make in order to "fit in" a white-dominated culture. I lived in a world of comfortable color-blindness. For me, and many of my colleagues, the fact that there were a few players of color scattered throughout the league was a real sign of progress. Good enough wasn't just good enough—it was great.

As Howard Bryant writes in *Full Dissidence: Notes from an Uneven Playing Field*, Fraser's conundrum is an all too familiar one, and only one that I, as a white writer, am beginning to understand. Bryant writes that even in the NBA and the NFL, Black athletes are tasked with assimilating to a white-dominant norm. If that's so, then the effect is multiplied in an NHL dressing room.

"The athlete is at the forefront of a certain type of trade: assimilation in exchange for money and star status affixed with serious conditions. The manifestations of such barter are especially chilling, for if Blackness cannot be expressed where Black people are dominant culturally and financially, what possible hope is there for African Americans in fields that they are not?"[6]

And hockey is definitely a "that they are not" kinda place.

Subban said that when he tried to express himself, it overshadowed the game. Trying to stand out, like how he dressed when he got off the team bus, always became the talking points. "I was going to be seen as a performer, as an entertainer, as flashy and loving the big moments," said Subban. "I don't know, I think I've had a pretty decent impact on the game, but that was a stigma that followed me, and it didn't matter what I did, I couldn't change it. And a lot of that was cultural.

"I never spoke about that during my career. To me, it wasn't a battle I wanted to pick. But it was always something that bothered me. I want to change that for the next generation of players."

That's why so many athletes of color find it hard to truly be themselves. Color outside the lines, just a little bit, and it impacts the way people see how you do your day job.

Bryant notes that being a professional athlete places players of color in a world dominated by white ticket-buyers. That's exponentially true in the world of hockey.

"The player who demands an answer places his or her entire professional career in jeopardy," writes Bryant. "More than ever, identifying as Black becomes a dangerous political choice."[7]

The rink is not just white-dominated, it is white, period. And that is something we all have to recognize, to shake ourselves from our color-blind ways.

SIX

GUILTY OF BEING WHITE

I **STOOD IN THE** Edmonton Oilers' Hall of Fame Room, the spot in Rogers Place where the team holds all of its major press conferences. It was filled with blue, orange, and copper memorabilia, with plaques dedicated to those very special Oilers who have been selected to the Hockey Hall of Fame.

It was early 2022, and at the podium was Evander Kane, who the Oilers had just signed that morning. The room was packed. When the Oilers make a signing, nothing else in Edmonton exists. It is *the* story of the day. Like many of the journalists in the press gallery, I waited for a member of the team's public relations staff to hand the microphone to me. I usually don't get antsy before I ask a question; after all, press conferences are old hat. But this time, I'd prepared a doozy.

"Evander, what would you say to the Oilers fans who aren't happy that you've signed with the team?"

It was a tough question, but a fair one. Kane's previous contract had been nullified by the San Jose Sharks. He had previously sought treatment for a gambling problem. He'd also been accused by his ex-wife of abuse, even though the courts had exonerated him and granted him custody of their child.

"I want to clear up a lot of the misinformation, a lot of the storylines painting me in a certain light that are completely untrue, inaccurate, and false," Kane responded. "I would encourage [fans] to be open minded, to allow me to do what I do best and get to know me on the ice, off the ice, around the rink, in the community, and see what I bring to the table.

"I take responsibility for things I've done wrong. But I'm definitely not taking responsibility for things I haven't done."[1]

To this day, I believe the question I asked him was tough, but fair. But as I write this book, I wonder—would I have asked the same hard question had Evander Kane been white?

Well, if any one of you out there would take the time to search my work to find out if I am full of shit or not, you'd know the answer. You might find a *Prague Post* article from 2003, where I spoke to Czech superstar Jaromir Jagr, right after he admitted he had accrued $450,000 USD in gambling debts and was more than $3 million in the hole to the Internal Revenue Service. I simply allowed him to change the subject when I brought it up—he wanted to speak instead about how he'd gone back to school in the summer to finish his degree in hotel management, fulfilling a promise he had made to his parents.

I let him off the hook.[2]

What I did was an example of what Irfan Chaudhry calls the "leniency effect."

What is the leniency effect? When the majority of the media and influencers around the game of hockey are white, when the wide majority of coaches and general managers are white, it's hard to break "similarity bias." That is, whites tend to be more forgiving and understanding of other whites.

The NHL—and the media—has a strong history of don't ask, don't tell. It is a league of second chances. And that, on the surface, is a very good thing.

There are some very significant examples of players who made comebacks. In 1984, then Boston Bruins forward Craig MacTavish killed twenty-six-year-old Kim Radley in a drunk-driving crash. He was sentenced to a year in prison after being convicted for vehicular homicide. MacTavish became a free agent in prison and signed with the Edmonton Oilers.

"The sentence isn't really over," MacTavish said when he was released. "It's not behind me. So many things remind me of my fatal mistake."[3]

MacTavish would go on to win three Stanley Cups with the Oilers and eventually became the team captain in 1992. He would win another Cup with the New York Rangers in 1994. He became a successful coach, leading the Oilers to the Cup final in 2006, and, eventually, a general manager.

It was a well-known unwritten rule in Edmonton that MacTavish's past was not to be brought up. He'd served his time, he's admitted his wrongdoing. He got his second chance, and he made the most of it. But ask yourself, would MacTavish have had as many doors open for him had he not been white, surrounded by white coaches, general managers, and media?

In 2003, Atlanta Thrashers star Dany Heatley was involved in a stunt-driving crash in his exotic European sports car. His Ferrari was traveling at about 80 miles per hour (130 km/h) when he lost control. His close friend and teammate, Dan Snyder, was killed in the crash. The Snyder family forgave Heatley publicly. In a 2005 Georgia court ruling, he received three years of probation after pleading guilty to second-degree vehicular homicide, driving too fast for the conditions, failure to maintain a lane, and speeding.

"This mistake will stay with me the rest of my life," Heatley said in court.[4]

Heatley restarted his career with the Ottawa Senators, and later played for the San Jose Sharks, Minnesota Wild, and the Anaheim Ducks. The Atlanta fans, like the Snyders, forgave Heatley, but the olive branches were burned when the player asked for a trade out of Georgia.

John Manasso documented the Heatley and Snyder family's journey in his book, *A Season of Loss, a Lifetime of Forgiveness*. When the book came out, he described the reaction from Atlanta fans to Heatley's trade request. "Even I was surprised at the visceral anger from some of the fans," Manasso said. "The fan base stood behind Dany. They gave him ovations when he returned. So, naturally, they felt like he rejected them."

First, we should ask the same question we'd pose to MacTavish—what would have happened had the player not been white? But there's another layer here that shows how white forgiveness works in sport—you can commit a crime, you can claim a life, but don't dare say you'd rather play somewhere else.

Kane has faced some serious allegations of abuse from his ex-wife, but a California court granted him custody of their child. The court demanded that Anna Kane needed to undergo psychiatric evaluations before being allowed supervised access to their child. Kane has had issues in the past—he's admitted his gambling problems, he declared bankruptcy, he was suspended by the NHL for breaking COVID protocols, and he had his contract dissolved by the San Jose Sharks. When he was signed by the Oilers in 2022, he told reporters that he almost got into a fight with Sharks assistant coach Rocky Thompson before that team ended his contract.

By no means am I suggesting that Kane has been a completely model citizen during his time in the NHL. But he faces constant scrutiny and media questions surrounding his past.

And, not to be too glib, he never killed anyone.

Chaudhry said that, in all sports, the media portrays white and Black athletes differently. During his presentation at the Grow the Game summit, he put up pictures of white superstars Connor McDavid and Sidney Crosby, and asked those watching what words came to mind. Then, he did the same after he put up pictures of Black NHL stars Kane and P. K. Subban.

Did the same words come to mind? Not likely.

That's because of built-in bias: Chaudhry said that, when white athletes are portrayed in the media, they're often credited for their smarts and hard work. When Black athletes are portrayed, their successes are usually credited for their physical attributes, and they can often be seen as "machine-like" in their desire to succeed.

"What type of biases might be fueling this?" Chaudhry asked his audience.[5] And he warned that those biases would fester in the coaches who make key decisions. "Who do we put out on the ice at certain times? Who we might not dress? Who we might not coach in similar ways?"

Subban enjoyed a stellar career. He was an alternate captain of the Montreal Canadiens, the most storied franchise in hockey. He won an Olympic gold medal with Team Canada in 2014 and won the Norris Trophy, which goes to the NHL's top defenseman, after the 2012–13 season. He retired in 2022. He's now a broadcaster with ESPN and the cochair of the NHL's Player Inclusion Coalition.

He admitted that he was really bothered by how he was portrayed as a player, but really has only become more comfortable talking about it since he hung up his skates. Subban was an offensive-minded defenseman, the kind of player who could start a rush up the ice, quarterback the power play, and thread the needle with his passes. He also played with intensity, and he recalls many of the great physical challenges that came with extended playoff runs.

But he wondered, even after he won the award that goes to the top defenseman in the NHL, why there were still so many articles that referred to him as a "high-risk" player. Google "Subban" and "high-risk," and what you'll get is page after page of articles. Subban isn't wrong—it was a brand that he hated, and it followed him wherever he went. If Subban turned a puck over, he wasn't forgiven.

"The tone in media is so important," said Subban. "I can remember some commentators and the way they'd say, 'Oh, P.K.'s gregarious,' and the words they'd use. But they'd never say that my skating ability was better than anyone else, he's going to have tons of energy. He's high-risk. It's like, that's skill and talent. It's not high-risk. If eight out of nine times, I'm making a play that works, that's not high-risk. High-risk is ten times you try it, and three times it works.

"I haven't seen a player in the league who is elite who hasn't turned a puck over, who hasn't made a mistake that's cost their team a game. It happens. When I did it, it was like a calling for everyone to pile on and wear this kid down so he doesn't have the confidence that he has."

What drove him nuts was that the same rules didn't apply to others. Hockey's culture of forgiveness had excluded Subban. "I saw so many players that came through the system that didn't have that talent, that didn't have that ability, given those opportunities," said Subban. "They were given second, third, fourth, fifth, and sixth chances, when they would cough up the puck and make mistakes. And, for some reason, I had the short leash."

Subban has plenty of admiration for contemporaries like Erik Karlsson and Drew Doughty, who were other star defensemen in the NHL during his heyday. The three players were compared to one another for the better part of a decade. Karlsson and Doughty were superstars and, like Subban, pushed the play to create some offense. Karlsson had years where his plus/minus (a measure of how many goals are scored by a player's team and the opposition when he's on the ice) was below −30. Karlsson and Subban were both named to the tournament all-star team after the completion of the 2008–09 World Juniors, so their careers will always be linked.

Doughty and Subban were both Norris Trophy finalists after the 2017–18 season. They were World Junior teammates for Team Canada. Doughty won Stanley Cups with the Los Angeles Kings in 2012 and 2014, but he suffered through a three-season spell from 2018–21 where he put up a cumulative –64 plus-minus rating. At even strength, he was on the ice for 64 more goals against than scored.

Now, this book is not designed to take shots at Karlsson and Doughty. Their successes on the ice far outweigh their flaws, and they will both be deserving members of the Hockey Hall of Fame when their time comes. But like all NHL players, they had flaws. It's just that they were never subjected to the same sorts of criticism as Subban. The media was far more lenient with the warts on their games.

"I look at players like Erik Karlsson. Drew Doughty. These are guys who play with offensive flair who never get called 'riverboat gamblers,'" said Subban. "The stuff that Erik Karlsson puts up with in terms of how people talk about his game is nothing compared to the way that people would talk about me—a guy who fought, who made big hits, who committed to a two-way style of play.

"I felt that, in hockey, everybody was trying to put me in this box. I believe a lot of that had to do with the culture of the game—it wasn't just based on my play and what I did on the ice. And that was tough to deal with. Now, you feel like the coach that's giving you criticism, the way people are talking about you in the media, is a little bit unfair."

In 2023, we once again saw white leniency in action. Bill Peters, the man who had racially abused Akim Aliu and lost his NHL coaching job—was back behind the bench in Alberta.

In late August, the Lethbridge Hurricanes, an elite junior team in the Western Hockey League, announced that Peters was being brought in as the head coach. A coach of a junior team not only stewards teenage prospects on the ice but is expected to be a mentor. And Hurricanes general manager Peter Anholt said, as he introduced Peters to the media, that the team is a "players first" organization.

When Peters stood behind the podium to meet the press, he broke down in tears.

"I now recognize the impact of my words," Peters said, sobbing. "I was uneducated in my use of inappropriate language. I take ownership of my actions, and regret my choice of words. I failed to create a safe place for Akim. I am deeply sorry. I am humbled about the opportunity to return to coaching in the Western Hockey League and the Lethbridge Hurricanes. It is a first-class organization in a world-class league."

As a term of his employment, Peters had to agree to "undergo continued equity and diversity training" under the supervision of the Western Hockey League, Hurricanes' management, and the equity consulting firm Shades of Humanity.

An unnamed NHL coach had tried to bring Aliu and Peters together to talk. But Aliu took to social media to let the world know how he felt about the situation. "It's been 13 years since the incident happened and four years since it's become public, I am curious as to why he wants to apologize now. Most folks don't know the back story of all that transpired. After the incident happened, instead of apologizing, he did everything in his power to blackball me in the game for over a decade. He even went as far as write a letter to Chicago management at the time stating it was either me or him, further alienating me from all of management."

Aliu noted that five members of the Blackhawks' management team would become general managers at clubs around the league; he believed that the Chicago diaspora helped word spread about him as a bad influence in the dressing room. At the time, he thought he had to "suck it up" in order to have any hope of having a pro career.

"It's something I could never recover from, and hockey was everything to me and my family." Aliu said he supported anyone, even Peters, having a second chance, "but only if they are sincere."

At the Lethbridge press conference, Peters said he wanted to meet with Aliu and formally apologize, eye to eye. He said the reason it had taken years for him to want to speak to his victim is that he had to learn a lot more about diversity and inclusion to really understand the impact of his transgressions.

"In order to make a proper apology, you have to be educated enough to do that…I'm much more comfortable in being able to craft that apology and have that conversation."

Just weeks after Peters was hired, more headlines about race and the old hockey guard came out of the Western Hockey League. Kevin Constantine had been hired to coach the Wenatchee Wild, an expansion team based in Washington State. Constantine was just another example of how old coaches can always bounce back. They can always be recycled. He had been a long-standing NHL coach. He coached superstar Jaromir Jagr in Pittsburgh in the late 1990s. He then coached eight seasons of junior hockey in Everett, Washington, in two separate stints.

Before Wenatchee had played a regular-season game, the league suspended Constantine and opened an investigation into his off-ice conduct. The league stated Constantine made "derogatory comments of a discriminatory nature." He was fired by the team in October 2023.

At the same time as the Constantine drama played out, controversy brewed in another Western Hockey League city, Red Deer in Alberta. The Red Deer Rebels, the very team that sent Arshdeep Bains on his path toward the NHL, named Kai Uchacz their team captain. As a member of the Seattle Thunderbirds, Uchacz missed the entire 2021–22 season after news broke of his racist behavior aimed at his Black teammate, Mekai Sanders. Uchacz spent time getting counseling from Shades of Humanity—the same group that worked with Peters—and eventually returned to the WHL. He was never drafted by an NHL team, but the Rebels decided to make him captain in 2023, making him the leader in the dressing room and a focal point for the media.

"I take full responsibility for my actions and I deeply regret my decision-making in the past," Uchacz was quoted in a WHL release when the league allowed the trade from Seattle to Red Deer to go through. "I have taken this time away from hockey to learn and grow as a person and have expanded my knowledge about this topic and how impactful it is. I thank the WHL for taking the time to work with me and believe in me as a person. I am thankful for the opportunity to play again."

But Sanders's agent, Scott Norton, said he and his client were "disappointed" that the league never officially handed down any discipline. Uchacz's one-year exile from hockey was of his own choosing, not because the league issued a suspension. On the books, he never received an official rebuke for the Sanders incidents.

A magical polygraph machine that can test people for their actual level of contrition, that strips away the layers of public relations bullshit and ignores the platitudes offered at press conferences, well, that hasn't been invented yet. What's clear is how we as whites are all too willing to not only move on but close the book once we do. While we see ourselves as virtuous, we are absolutely ignorant of how insincere we look to others. The road to redemption should be rocky—but when it comes to the leniency effect, we've created a smooth, paved road with only green lights along the way.

THE MEDIA

It is the longest-running prime-time sports show on the planet—in fact, it's so old that it began as a radio show. It makes *Monday Night Football* look like a kid in diapers. And it's hard to find any sports program, anywhere, that is so ingrained in a country's psyche.

It is *Hockey Night in Canada*. For Canadians, *HNIC* is a Saturday night ritual that goes back generations. From Foster Hewitt to Danny Gallivan to Bob Cole to Jim Hughson, the voices that called the game provided the soundtracks to the lives of Canadians, from a time when cars had fins and hood ornaments bigger than human heads.

But one voice was louder than anyone else on *Hockey Night in Canada*—and really, sets the tone for hockey broadcasting throughout North America. And that was Don Cherry. A man who had a long-standing minor-hockey career, played a total of one NHL game, and then went on to be a coach most famous for putting too many on the ice and potentially costing his Boston Bruins a Stanley Cup.

For almost four decades, *Coach's Corner* was appointment viewing in Canada. If you were in the press box for a Saturday night game, you got up from your seat to gather with your fellow media members around the nearest TV so you could all watch what Don had to say.

He was the king of the watercooler. He'd speak of "beautiful" Canadian players, as shots of teams entering the rinks, decked in suits and ties, played on the screen. He'd chastise Canadians, especially immigrants, for not doing enough to honor our military. He praised the fighters, and woe to any player he viewed as "soft." Saturday night was his platform to name names—and to call out players he didn't see as meeting the code. Woe to European players, for taking away jobs from North Americans. If a North American player fought, Cherry lauded him as tough. If a European player showed any physical prowess on the ice, he was dirty and dangerous.

Cherry's voice grew to the point where political parties—both on the left and right—approached him to run for office.

Then in 2019, CBC and Sportsnet, who co-aired *HNIC*, pulled the plug on Cherry after his Remembrance Day rant targeted a wrong that did not exist. Cherry, who for years had screamed that Canada allowed too many immigrants into the country, went on a tirade about how newcomers didn't respect veterans because they didn't wear poppies on their lapels to mark Remembrance Day.

"You people that come here, you love our way of life, you love our milk and honey, at least you can pay a couple of bucks for poppies or something like that," he yelled into his lapel mic.

You people. Cherry had been inflaming Canadians since 1982, but those two words were too much. Cherry was axed.

Chaudhry believes that Cherry created a special leniency effect in hockey, where even whites were separated culturally. Canadians and Americans were treated differently in pro hockey than players from Sweden, Finland, what was then Czechoslovakia—and then later the Russians. From this, Chaudhry thinks North American white hockey fans and players can learn a lot. If at one time, they saw Swedes and Finns as the "other," maybe they can take that as a jumping-off point. If breaking into North American hockey was hard for white Europeans, how hard must it be for players with different colors of skin?

"There are so many examples where North American players were given more leniency or the perception of leniency than European players in terms of chances to succeed," Chaudhry said.

The soft Swede. The dirty Finn. These are tropes that existed through the 1980s and 1990s. If you still need to be convinced that race is an issue in hockey, take the first step. Think about how *Coach's Corner* turned whites against whites.

It's easy to roll up all of hockey's baggage and blame Cherry for it all. But Cherry didn't create the *Hockey Night in Canada* culture. He simply followed the pattern. To say that Cherry was *HNIC*'s sole lightning rod would be as ridiculous as saying that Elvis invented rock 'n' roll.

HNIC has always been about celebrating the players from small towns across Canada. It celebrates the kids that came from places like Aneroid or Kelvington or Flin Flon or Terrace Bay. Yet, for decades it was an unflinchingly white institution. There were no people of color to be found anywhere near the studio or the broadcast booth.

It was also the blueprint that American hockey broadcasters used. Barry Melrose, the mulleted former coach of the Los Angeles Kings, became the de facto Cherry south of the border.

The whiteness of the media—and the whiteness of the narratives—wasn't lost on Anson Carter when he played in the NHL. "I'll give you an example. Playing in Edmonton, they love their Western Canadian boys. You always hear about the Western Canadian boys out west, which is amazing."

He didn't have an issue with the "good farm boy" narrative. To him, the issue was that it was the *only* narrative. And he wondered why he or his family was never asked to talk about their story, where they came from, and how they fit into the idea of what it meant to be Canadian.

"How come no one says this about me and my family?" Carter said. "My parents came to Toronto from Barbados in 1967. They were given nothing. They didn't have two nickels to rub together. But they were able to raise three kids, and all of us went to university, went to college, good lives, good jobs, great citizens, son plays in the National Hockey League. How come that isn't described as a good character person? So, now being a person of color on TV, I can talk about that. I think that's important to attract a new audience."

Carter and Subban are now fixtures on broadcasts in both the United States and Canada. Carter is on TNT and Sportsnet. Subban is an analyst for ESPN. Former Canadian and American women's national-team players are now in front of the cameras. While change is slow, it's important.

That's because of how media impacts the coaches and administrators who work with kids. Chaudhry said that, when a child enters minor hockey for the first time, that kid's first mentor will be a volunteer coach. Hockey in both the United States and Canada needs volunteers to make it all work, from coaches to team managers to parents who carpool their kids to tournaments. And they don't have the professional training needed to at least confront their biases.

He also said almost all of these volunteers get their hockey knowledge through the media. So, imagine the effects of the "good farm boy" narrative on a white coach. It's powerful. In Canada, Rogers aired *Hometown Hockey* broadcasts from 2014–22, which were generally hosted in hockey-mad hotspots across Canada. NHLers who hail from the area guested on the show. Images of minor-hockey kids played in the background.

Once a year, *Hockey Day in Canada* is celebrated by Rogers and CBC. The NHL schedules the Canadian clubs to play one another for a triple-header of games, and the whole day is hosted from a hockey hot-bed. Both *Hockey Day in Canada* and *Hometown Hockey* are easy examples of ready-made Canadiana, spoon-fed to the masses, and it often perpetuates that farm-boy-making-it-to-the-NHL stereotype. It took five years for *Hockey Day in Canada* to host a broadcast from a First Nation.

TV, though, is driven by one thing—numbers. As Davis preaches, racial equity as a business decision is a more powerful notion than racial equity because it's the right thing to do. More viewers equal more sponsor dollars. There is very little altruism left in sports broadcasting.

During the 2008 Stanley Cup playoffs, CBC launched a Punjabi language version of *Hockey Night in Canada*. There are nearly one million Punjabi Canadians, and they represent a massive, untapped market. (Remember that Canada's population is about one-eighth of the United States, so a million people is a big deal north of the border.) During the 2016 Cup final between the Pittsburgh Penguins and the San Jose Sharks, play-by-play man Harnarayan Singh—who was raised in the only Sikh family in the town of Brooks, Alberta, became a cult hero for the call of Nick Bonino's Game 1–winning goals. His *BoninoBoninoBoninoBoninoBoninoNickBoniiiiiinoooooooo* clip went viral and became the soundtrack to the Penguins' Cup win. Singh moved to the English language *Hockey Night in Canada* broadcasts in 2019.

Singh was not the first person of color to call a hockey game in North America. But the Punjabi broadcasts broke down a major barrier, taking the telecasts out of the Franco-Anglo norm. It opened the door for broadcasts in other languages—since the Punjabi format debuted, there have been national Cree broadcasts in Canada as well. In 2021, Sportsnet offered games in Cantonese, Mandarin, Hindi, Vietnamese, Tagalog, Arabic, and German as a test. But this was a product of a business decision, to expand the broadcasts to an underserved population.

Change in hockey broadcasting is slow. But it's necessary. Representation isn't just about what happens on the ice.

"It is critical," Davis said of the need to see more faces of color in the broadcast booths and press boxes. "It is one of those levers. When you are looking to improve something, there's not one path to that improvement. In the case of our sport, there are multiple cylinders that have to be pulled, and one of the most critical ones is representation. And that's representation on the ice, that's representation in media, that's representation in the locker room and the front office. When you have represented voices around the table or on the ice, it brings a different perspective.

"To be clear, we have different conversations around [commissioner Gary Bettman]'s table with Heidi Browning [the NHL's chief marketing officer] and I there, just because we are representing a different experience, a different point of view, a different way of looking at the world."

Carter remembers how the media spoke and wrote about him during his playing days, and that drives him when he's behind the mic at Sportsnet and TNT. "I learned a lot about the power of the microphone. There were times when I was a free agent and I'd hear all these stories coming out—Carter's not *focused*. I remember when I was in LA—oh, he's not *focused*. He's worried about his entertainment company, living in California. He's hanging out in Hollywood. Meanwhile, I was training with [Chris] Chelios and Rob Blake and [Alexander] Mogilny, some of the top players in the game, but no one was talking about that. They were talking about Anson living in California and having Louis Vuitton on in his car and stuff like that. It was the kind of craziness that would make me laugh because the same people talking trash would probably puke if they had to do the 7 a.m. workouts that we were doing out there in Venice, California, every single day. I learned that the media has a very powerful presence, whether it's right or wrong, and I've learned how important it is to correct the way the game is seen by everybody."

Subban retired at the age of thirty-three, and it came as a surprise to the hockey world. But when he made the decision that he wasn't coming back, he got a call from Penguins superstar Sidney Crosby, who told him that hockey needed Subban to remain involved in the game at some level.

Crosby's Penguins beat Subban's Nashville Predators in the 2017 Cup final. "He stole my Stanley Cup," Subban joked; in truth, he relished every time he got to battle against the best player of the generation. So having Crosby reach out and ask Subban to remain plugged into the NHL meant a lot.

But Subban doesn't want to be just another hockey talking head who overuses and misuses the word "unbelievable" and gets paid to state the obvious.

"I wanted to rectify a lot of the wrongs. Not just for Black players, but for all players. I think that hockey players have had to deal with a lot in the media. Because of the culture, everybody is so tight-lipped. As a player, you don't always get the chance to express yourself about how you feel about yourself. I wanted to be an added voice for the players. And a lot of that had to come with these talking points—I know what it's like to deal with the culture of the game. I've lived it. I'm willing to sit down with any analyst, any person working in TV in hockey, and having a discussion on any topic. And I think they know that.

"This is a huge topic for me on why I got into the media in the first place. I got involved because I was so sick and tired of these guys not doing the work. Sometimes, I believe it wasn't people doing their job and doing their research. Watching the games. Knowing the players. Getting feedback from people. It's not about going and talking to their hockey buddies and coming up with who they want to support and who they don't want to support. So, I definitely felt inclined to send that message that I was going to be someone who worked in the media. The driving component for me is that if you really want to change something, then get involved. Don't sit on the sidelines, this is your opportunity to get involved, to get in the game."

Here's a modern example of why hockey's media corps needs to be less, well, white.

The Oilers got off to an unexpected, poor start to the 2023–24 season. During an intermission interview, Evander Kane noted that he got into a second-period fight after he "didn't play much in the first period." That led to a full-on discussion by the all-white *Hockey Night in Canada* panel. Was Kane throwing then coach Jay Woodcroft under the bus? How dare a player break the "code" and complain about his ice time? It was so... un-*Canadian*!

But was it a big deal? ESPN and TSN's Kevin Weekes was the first media person to come to Kane's defense—a Black man defending a Black man in a sea of white outrage.

"When a player wants more, I don't have a problem with that," Weekes said.

That's the thing. All Kane suggested was that he wanted to play more. If there is a pro athlete out there who wants less ice time or field time or court time, I've yet to meet that person. There isn't a backup quarterback in the NFL who doesn't want to be a starter. And every coach wants to know that players are unhappy when playing time is reduced.

Nothing Kane said was a big deal, at all. But a Black player suggesting he wanted to do more for his team? *Whoa.*

"In the media, in our sport, we have to have these voices, because they become myth-busters," said Davis. "They can say, 'What's the big deal?' Then, it goes away. The more we have of that, the more we normalize differences. Then we don't have to keep talking about it."

And the Kane incident? According to Davis, "it demonstrates just how deeply rooted this idea of hockey culture is."

There certainly are many examples of white outrage and pushback when it comes to advancing the discussion of equity in hockey. But the example I'm ending this chapter with stands above and beyond in terms of running not to aid the victim of racism but to offer sympathy to the white figure who perpetrated the racism.

Here we go…

THE GREYHOUNDS AND THE CULTURE

Communities across North America are divided when it comes to the takedown of banners or statues that allow whites to forgive themselves for historical wrongs, *because that's how all people thought back then.* It's OK to glorify the political advances of this slave owner because, well, *people thought differently about slavery in 1850.* Why should we change the name of this street? Sure, the man who it's named for helped create the residential school system, but really all *he wanted to do was help Indigenous people in the only way he knew how.*

Close to downtown, there's an Edmonton neighborhood that had been known as Oliver for decades. It was named for Frank Oliver, who, late in the nineteenth century, was the most-well-known newspaperman in the city and later became an elected member of parliament and government minister. Despite being the overseer of Indian Affairs early in the twentieth century, Oliver was already well known for pushing the agenda of white settlers' rights. He was an equal-opportunity bigot because his public scorn and powers of public office were also used to hamper the efforts of Black Americans who had looked to immigrate to Canada. He publicly compared Chinese immigrants to pigs and said that Slavic immigrants could never become full-fledged Canadian citizens. *But he was just like a lot of white leaders at the time, right?*

His name lived on for generations, all because, well, he was a city builder. A government minister. A famed journalist. But the community league in Oliver began efforts in 2020 to change the name, issuing a public statement that "Frank Oliver spearheaded many harmful policies that directly targeted Indigenous communities, people of color, newcomers, and people with disabilities. This namesake does not reflect the spirit of diversity and inclusion that our community represents."

In early 2024, a new name was picked for the community—wîhk-wêntôwin. It's a Cree word, meaning "circle of friends." This was widely endorsed by members of the community. The people spoke, and the change was made. Still, there were opponents, warning that it was yet another example of erasing history. There were complaints that the new word was just too difficult to pronounce, despite the fact that Canada is filled with place names derived from Indigenous languages.

It's just one example of the place-name debates that are happening around North America right now. My alma mater, Toronto's once-named Ryerson University, is now Toronto Metropolitan University. The former namesake, nineteenth-century educator Egerton Ryerson, was also a massive supporter of the divisive residential school program that is now one of Canada's greatest shames.

Christopher Columbus did not "discover" America—there were already civilizations here when he arrived. Washington and Jefferson may have preached freedom, but surely had little issue with slavery. Heck, Washington asked the Brits to return the slaves who fought with the Loyalists during the Revolution.

Sure, there are those who argue that tearing down monuments and changing the names of communities and streets scrubs away our history. Yet, the history books won't change. Every kid should learn about slave owners and Nazis and apartheid and humankind's incredible ability to segregate and oppress one another. But while the books will still tell us about racial discrimination and Nazis and Valley Forge and the Last Spike, how we view that history should evolve and change. It's part of being human. Why not honor those who fought against oppression rather than the oppressors? It's a simple shift to make, no?

Crystal M. Fleming succinctly rebuts the "but we have to understand racism in its historical context" crowd in her book *How to Be Less Stupid About Race*: "Others will object and say that condemning the founders for their moral crimes against humanity is unfair, because it means using our current values to judge historical figures. But this narrative—long dominant (and typically invoked by white men)—deliberately ignores the fact that people spoke out against and opposed white supremacist genocide and chattel slavery *while these things were happening*."[6] If we can apply that thinking to how we judge historical figures, it should be less of a leap to use that to judge the game.

How do we frame Conn Smythe, one of the great builders of the game, the man who built Maple Leaf Gardens, but who also had a history of racial and religious prejudices? We shouldn't be afraid to call him a racist—he watched Herb Carnegie skate in the very arena he owned, and dismissed the man based on the color of his skin.

How do we reconcile the fact that the promise of organized hockey was used by the superintendents of residential schools to falsely give the impression that they were looking out for the best interests of Indigenous kids? They absolutely weren't, and we have to understand how hockey was used as a tool to dominate Canada's first people.

More importantly, the very presences of Carnegie and Kwong, playing in arenas that had previously been reserved for white men, daring to dream of playing in the NHL, were major acts of opposition to the white norm of professional hockey in the 1930s and 1940s. They didn't need to write manifestos or lead town hall meetings to argue against the status quo; they did it by simply daring to dream. So, Fleming's point is proven within the hockey context; there were people who openly defied the white supremacist way that the game was run. And they had those who supported them, too; Punch Imlach, the coach and general manager of the Quebec Aces, arguably the best-known minor pro team in Canada, signed Carnegie and his brother, Ossie, and Manny McIntyre to become the first all-Black line in hockey since the days of the Colored Hockey League. He later signed O'Ree and his close friend, Stan Maxwell.

In some cases, the statues are coming down—but not without a fight from the old guard of the culture.

This brings me back to Sault Ste. Marie, Ontario. Late in 2023, the Greyhounds of the Ontario Hockey League decided to take down the banner honoring John Vanbiesbrouck, the American goalie who would go on to play 882 career games with the New York Rangers, Florida Panthers, Philadelphia Flyers, New York Islanders, and New Jersey Devils. In 2018, he was named the assistant executive director of hockey operations for USA Hockey, a position he still held as of the writing of this book.

Let's back up to 2003. Vanbiesbrouck was back on the Canadian side of the border, coaching and managing the Greyhounds. He was also a part owner of the club. It seemed like poetry, an American hockey legend returning to the Canadian junior side where he'd first really made his name. But Vanbiesbrouck left the team after using the N-word several times to describe and denigrate one of his players, Trevor Daley. The incident led to Vanbiesbrouck's resignation—and he divested himself of his share in the team for which he once starred.

Still, a banner that celebrated Vanbiesbrouck's junior hockey career hung from the rafters. But during the 2023–24 season, it was quietly removed. There was no fanfare. It was just…gone.

Daley, who played 1,058 NHL games, made this statement through the Hockey Diversity Alliance: "The one dark and very racist moment of my hockey career is something I had to relive each time I returned to the Gardens and looked up to the rafters. The next time I enter the Gardens, look up, and not have to relive one of the worst moments of my life eliminates a major source of anger and frustration for both me and my family."

Daley issued this statement on January 30, 2024, two weeks after Sault Ste. Marie newspaper columnist Doug Millroy suggested that Vanbiesbrouck was the real victim. It was a clear case of white blame-shifting that we so often see when people who look like me are confronted with calls of racism. We act like we're the injured party, and that the embarrassment and shame is a punishment that doesn't fit our crime. We're sorry for our bigotry, so why do we have to wear it?

Millroy's column was the equivalent of killing a bug not with a hammer, but with a thermonuclear weapon. He decided to invoke one of the city's most notorious killings, the slaying and dismemberment of drug dealer Wesley Hallam, in order to make his case that it was Vanbiesbrouck and not Daley who deserved our sympathies. Hallam's killers had their charges controversially scaled down to manslaughter, because of the amount of alcohol and drugs involved, and the slaying occurring after a knife fight. Each of the perpetrators got twelve years in jail.

"Twenty years after the Daley incident I have to ask, how long does Vanbiesbrouck have to pay for it, forever?" wrote Millroy.[7] "Eric Mearow, Ronald Mitchell and Dylan Jocko, the three who beheaded Wesley Hallam, were free and clear in 12.

"Simply put, I am convinced the Greyhounds made a mistake in removing Vanbiesbrouck's jersey. Surely a man should not be defined in perpetuity by a wrongful and hurtful comment he made in a heated moment.

"And where does forgiveness stand in all this? Shouldn't it be taken into account? After all, nobody died."

Wow. Sometimes, that's the only word that works. Comparing the removal of a commemorative banner to a killing? As white indignation goes, this deserves Hall of Fame mention. And the Greyhounds did not unretire Vanbiesbrouck's No. 1 jersey. He's still honored on the team's website. Basically, the team's ownership did the bare minimum twenty years after the Daley/Vanbiesbrouck incident.

Just a couple of months after the banner came down, former Greyhounds goaltender Tucker Tynan launched a $300,000 lawsuit against the team, claiming that he was subjected to racial slurs and forced to play through a shoulder injury. The statement of claim, which, as of the writing of this book, has yet to be proven in a court of law, alleged that the team's staff elected not to take him to the hospital when he had to leave a game in April 2022. The claim stated that Tynan later told management about the constant pain he suffered, but his pleas for help were met with derogatory language. In its statement of defense submitted in court, the team stated that its officials had "imperfect knowledge" of

Tynan's injuries that the plaintiff's claims were "replete with false and inflammatory allegations, the motivations for which the Greyhounds, at this time, can only speculate."[8]

What did Davis say about hockey's culture being "deeply rooted?" Time to drop the mic on this chapter.

SEVEN

THE CULTURE OF SILENCE

IN A WORLD filled with social media faux pas, a single tweet from the Vegas Golden Knights account (or is that xeet, now?) stood out for its simplicity—and perfection. It was *the* post that should have been flagged for the PR departments of the thirty-one other teams in the league. It should have been a screenshot that was sent around the league.

The tweet/xeet contained a video taken from the grounds of the Sioux Valley Dakota Nation in southern Manitoba, a little more than a ninety-minute drive from the American border. The sounds of drums can be heard. Steady. Powerful. Whoops and hollers provide the rest of the soundtrack as a crowd gathers on the grounds.

And there it comes, the Stanley Cup. Held by Zach Whitecloud, the kid who left Sioux Valley to pursue his dream of making it to the NHL. Not only did he realize that dream, he's a champion.

This is one thing hockey does better than any of the other "Big Four" American sports. The trophy.

The NBA's Larry O'Brien Championship Trophy and the NFL's Lombardi Trophy are the stuff of gift shop chic, easily copied and unremarkable. Wow, a trophy that has a basketball, and another in the shape of a football. Wow, really thought outside the box with those ones, all right. The World Series Commissioner's Trophy, with its circle of pennants, is a little better. And it gets worse—the tacky trophies are handed out in the tackiest of fashions. When an MLB, NBA, or NFL team wins a championship, the commissioner of said league will then hand the trophy to the owner of the triumphant franchise—a needless salute to the hubris of wealthy white men.

But the Stanley Cup is different. The original Cup resides permanently in the Hockey Hall of Fame, as it is too delicate and brittle to be regularly handled. The Cup that's currently handed out is made not of gold but of silver and nickel alloy. It's like if you took a lot of spare change, melted it down, and reforged it into a trophy.

That Cup, though, carries the history of the game. Every player on a Cup-winning team gets his name engraved on it. When the Cup is full, the oldest barrel band is carefully removed and preserved in the Hockey Hall of Fame. And when the Cup is won, the commissioner hands the trophy not to some old owner but to the team captain to hold aloft. The captain then passes to a teammate, he does a victory lap with it, and then it's passed on to another—until every winning player has touched it.

The off-season is a busy one for the winning team. It is tradition for each member of the Stanley Cup–winning team to get one day with the trophy. The players bring the Cup to their hometowns or places that are special to them. It's been to the top of mountains, it's been filled with a variety of drinks, it's been the de facto prize in a road-hockey tournament. It's been tossed into a swimming pool.

The video of Whitecloud's day with the Cup was posted on social media on the Knights account in 2023. There were no words in the caption, just an orange heart. Orange is the color of reconciliation—for Indigenous people, it stands for justice, for education, for understanding.

Whitecloud uses his status as a defenseman for one of the top teams in the league as a platform to help fans across North America better understand the painful history of Indigenous people in Canada.

While Las Vegas has become his home, he is deeply connected to his roots, and he shares that connection with the thousands of fans who follow his social media accounts. He believes that he can use his celebrity for good and educate young fans in both Canada and the United States about the Indigenous history they were never taught in school.

Canada's non-Indigenous population has only begun its journey of understanding. In the nineteenth century (and well into the twentieth), Canadian governments saw Indigenous children not as civilized humans born into loving, caring families, but as savages. So for generations, Indigenous kids were ripped from their families, stolen from their communities, and whisked away to "residential schools" that were located across the country. Often, the promise of playing organized hockey was used as a lure to make kids more willing to be taken from their families.

Abuse was common in these schools. Kids were stripped of their names. Any attempts at preserving their Indigenous languages or cultures were met with brutal punishments. Many children disappeared—researchers and historians are only beginning to tally the number of dead. Sophisticated archaeological equipment has been used to scan the grounds of former residential schools, and there have been some grisly finds, including 215 anomalies at one former residential school site in Kamloops, British Columbia (see chapter 2).

But none of this got into Canadian history books. Sure, there was some mention of residential schools, but the versions that were taught in grade-nine social studies classes were stripped of the brutal details. That is changing, but there are swaths of people across North America who barely have any knowledge of Canada's greatest shame.

In the summer of 2022, Pope Francis made an official visit to Canada, and, after visiting the site of the Ermineskin Indian Residential School in Maskwacis, Alberta, he issued this apology to the thousands of people who had gathered to hear him speak, and to the media representing outlets from around the world.

"I am here because the first step of my penitential pilgrimage among you is that of again asking forgiveness, of telling you once more that I am deeply sorry," said the pope. "Sorry for the ways in which, regrettably, many Christians supported the colonizing mentality of the powers that oppressed the Indigenous peoples. I am sorry."

Whitecloud lives with the lingering pain of residential schools. He has family members who were forced into the residential school system. He saw the trauma that continues to shroud communities like his.

So, why not use his celebrity to tell people about it?

This is what he wrote on Instagram on September 30, 2022, Canada's National Day for Truth and Reconciliation:

> Reconciliation requires truth, sincerity, and accountability for our words and actions. Reconciliation requires leadership and our individual efforts to speak the truth, and acknowledge truth so that we can build a foundation for a relationship. It is our responsibility to be informed and to actively participate in addressing the genocide, the pain and suffering, to commit to a new relationship built on trust.
>
> My grandfather, grandmother, and uncle are all residential school survivors. We are still here, to heal, educate, and move forward on the right path—a positive direction.
>
> We will not forget the pain and suffering, the disrespect, to be treated as less than human. We will gain strength from the resiliency of our relatives who survived, and we will honor their sacrifices. My grandfather, grandmother, and uncle have paid the price of resiliency, and we will honor them and many others by thriving, by excelling and by never forgetting the sacrifices of those who paved the way for us.
>
> Learn, educate, read and share stories, put forth an effort to understand our people's past and present issues. Together, we can move forward.[1]

Whitecloud said he's also been able to start conversations with his Golden Knights teammates about this part of Canada's history that's been glossed over for too long. "It's not something we learned in school growing up, right?" said Zach in an interview I did with him before the Knights won the Cup in 2023. "I am in a scenario where I can use the things that I've learned and relay that to my friends and teammates. I am always open to talking about it. It comes with educating people who were never educated about this. That's important—knowing the severity of what's happened, what our people, my ancestors, what they had to go through. And it's not so far removed, I have close family members who experienced those things. A lot of people believe that it's history, but it's not. It's alive today. The traumas and the hurt that people went through. A lot of our elders and ancestors live with those experiences, today.

"Having those conversations is sometimes the thing that moves the needle forward in the direction that it needs to go. I am never going to speak for anyone who went through it, but those things can't be reconciled. It's difficult to grasp that this has happened in your own country. It's something that happened in your country and no one is talking about it, in depth. It's what I tell other people—the thing that I've been taught from my aunts and uncles and others from the community is that you can never really relay how those people felt. You can never truly understand how those people felt. It's incomprehensible. It rips away the identity of how people live, the way you feed your family, the way you pray. It was all ripped away by people who lived amongst you in your own country. So, sharing any information I know, that's important. It's important to learn. It's important to educate. I've reiterated this in my posts—it's not to point blame...it's about allowing people access to learn and to understand what's happened in the past."

He thanks his father, Tim, for helping him understand that having a platform is something he simply could not turn down.

"It comes from my parents. When you start moving up levels, then into pro hockey, and then the ultimate goal of playing in the NHL, a lot of eyes are on you, not just as an Indigenous person. But you add my background, you have a lot of people looking up to you, people tuning into games when they normally wouldn't, to watch one of their own people playing. I learned a lot from my dad specifically; he kept reiterating that I had this platform, a voice I can use to move things in a positive direction. I am trying to use that platform the best that I can, to promote my culture, our people, and the way that we live. I do understand the importance of moving things forward in a positive direction, our culture, our practices, the history of my people. There are so many important things to be shared and learned."

Whitecloud is using sport to help create better understanding of the Indigenous nations that existed in North America centuries before any white settlers "discovered" this land. It's a refreshing and needed change because, for generations, sports were used to amplify negative stereotypes—and it's still happening now. Sure, after much public pressure, the Edmonton Eskimos, Washington Redskins, and Cleveland Indians changed their names. But there are still fans who go to Kansas City Chiefs games and feel that banging on war drums and performing a pantomime of a tomahawk chop is OK. It's hard to reconcile; players take a knee to protest the treatment of Blacks in America, but then chop to celebrate a touchdown. If the Atlanta Braves have runners in scoring position, we're sure to hear fans join in one of the cringiest traditions in sport: the war cry and "tomahawk chop."

In his memoir, Fred Sasakamoose, the first full treaty Indigenous player in the NHL, recalled that when he played in the major junior leagues for the Moose Jaw Canucks, an arrangement was made to have a Cree naming ceremony in Edmonton, before a game against the Oil Kings. It's a sacred thing; Sasakamoose received the Cree title of Chief Running Deer, in honor of his skating skill. But the media quickly turned it into yet another example of how sports used Indigenous people as caricatures. Newspapers ran stories about Sasakamoose "scalping" the opposition. Or that Sasakamoose was on the "warpath."

He wrote: "The Edmonton team even ran an ad in the paper the following season with a headshot of one of their star players and the lines 'Will this man be scalped tomorrow night? Freddy Sasakamoose, Moose Jaw's Indian "whiz kid," is on the warpath as the Moose Jaw Canucks meet the Edmonton Oil Kings at the Gardens in another thrilling junior hockey engagement!'"[2]

It's hard to keep count of the number of Indigenous players who have had to endure the "chief" nickname.

Ted Nolan is an Ojibwe coach who grew up in Garden River, a First Nation in Northern Ontario. He would coach the Sault Ste. Marie Greyhounds to a Memorial Cup title before getting his shot in the NHL. Despite leading an injury-plagued and low-budget Buffalo Sabres team to a playoff spot in his second year, the headlines about him were about how he caused tumult in the front office. Rumors started circulating that he was drinking on the job. In 1997, he decided not to accept what he described as a lowball one-year contract extension offer from the Sabres, right after he won the Jack Adams, which goes to the NHL coach of the year. It would be nearly a decade before he coached in the NHL again. He couldn't help but wonder if racial profiling had played a part.

"Did other GMs and management really think I'd work to get them fired? That I was a 'GM killer?'" Nolan wrote.[3] "Did the hockey world really think I was irrationally hard-headed and impossible to work with? Did people really believe I'd been drunk at practices?"

It would be easy for Whitecloud to do as so many others have before, stick to sports. But to say Whitecloud is grounded would be an understatement. As a junior hockey player, he wasn't considered anything close to a top prospect. His story is one of perseverance—he earned a spot at Bemidji State University in Minnesota after being cut by two junior teams in Manitoba. He was never selected in the NHL draft, and he later signed with Vegas as a free agent out of school—these are the sorts of players who are brought into professional teams to fill out minor-league rosters, and that's about it.

But Whitecloud impressed in the Vegas system, and now is a regular part of the defensive corps. Coach Bruce Cassidy believes Whitecloud will be a strong NHL defenseman for years to come. "He's a really good young player for us, who's going to continue to get better," Cassidy said. "Over time, I think you'll see it down the road, I don't know when that will be, because some guys age out, he'll be a really good top-four defenseman in this league."

"The development path was a long route; it definitely wasn't linear, that's for sure," said Whitecloud. "A lot of ups and downs. I took a stop at every level besides major junior. It's been fun. No one from my inner circle or myself expected me to come this far, let alone college or the American Hockey League. Each day, you take experiences from it. Every day you play in this league, it's never a given, it's a privilege."

Whitecloud grew up in Brandon, Manitoba's second-largest city, but his roots are in the nearby Sioux Valley Dakota Nation. As he rose through the ranks, he needed financial help in order to play on teams that traveled. His Indigenous community stepped up—they helped subsidize the high cost of hockey. "They helped out with education, with sports, with hockey, anything the kids from the community want to try," Zach said. "And, if they're serious about it, they help out. They helped me out, and I'm forever grateful for it. Any contribution or show of support from them was just huge for me.

"It was more when I got a bit older and got onto the teams that traveled more, going away for tournaments, and staying overnight for games. Our community started to help out more, with me being the only person from the community playing travel hockey."

Growing up, he watched *Hockey Night in Canada* every Saturday night. But unlike most kids, he didn't have one player that stood out over the others in his mind. "We just watched *Hockey Night in Canada*, CBC, channel 3, whatever it was, and it was a case of whoever's playing that night. It was typically Toronto, Montreal, or Boston. Those were the games I watched. For me, I was a hockey fan. I didn't have a certain favorite player or a certain favorite team; I just loved the game."

During Vegas's run to the Stanley Cup in 2023, Whitecloud was placed in the middle of a media firestorm—because of his name.

In the second round of the playoffs, the Knights faced the Edmonton Oilers, and in Game 3 of the series, Whitecloud unleashed a wicked wrist shot that went over the shoulder of goalie Stuart Skinner and went in just under the crossbar. It was a perfect shot, one that would have beaten any NHL netminder. It made the highlight reels of the sports-wrap-up shows that aired across North America, and that included *Sportscenter*, ESPN's flagship show. John Anderson, the host of the show, decided some humor was needed when describing Whitecloud's goal. He suggested that Whitecloud was a "great name if you're a toilet paper [brand]."

Quickly, Anderson realized that this was going to be something he'd need to address. By now, most of the general public recognizes that making fun of someone's name—no matter their culture or background—is something that we might hear in grade school, and at that point we work with the kids to make them understand that it's insensitive and wrong. For adults, to quote a famous NFL pregame segment: come on, man.

Anderson spoke to Whitecloud, and then the defenseman told reporters that he'd forgiven the ESPN anchor. In keeping with how he's conducted himself in the past, Zach used it as a teaching moment. "I'm proud of my culture, I'm proud of where I come from, where I was raised," said Zach. "I carry my grandfather's last name, and nothing makes me more proud than to be able to do that. I believe [Anderson] was sincere in his apology and I was going to be the first person to reach out my hand and offer help. People make mistakes, right? And it's a time for everyone to learn."

And of course, Whitecloud's name is now immortalized on a band of the best trophy in sports.

Whitecloud's outspokenness makes him a rarity in the NHL. Dressing rooms in the NHL are closed places, and players are very guarded about what they say. In fact, there are many nights where it's hard to find anything quotable in the dressing room. We in the media are complicit because our questions often stay within some rigid lines. And if an athlete is outspoken outside the rink, we in the very white hockey media stick to sport when we don't need to. Indeed, we use the word "media" to describe ourselves a lot more than we're willing to call ourselves "journalists." It's like the weight of the mighty j-word is too much when we can instead talk about penalty-killing percentage and the need to try to find left-shooting defensemen at the trade deadline.

The thought of a journalist asking Alexander Ovechkin about his outspoken support of Vladimir Putin…it's just not something that happens.

There is an unwritten rule in hockey that what goes on in the room, stays in the room. When the media arrives in the dressing room after the game, the players aren't there. That's a big difference from twenty years ago, when reporters could search players out in the room.

They've cleared out of their stalls. Three or four players are brought out, one by one, by PR staff. The team's own media teams are there in the scrums, which removes the motivation for the independent press to be candid in their questions. Writers are practically giving away their angles when their questions are being broadcast live to teams' social media accounts—and it gives an average fan the feeling that the newspaper writers and teams aren't in a state of healthy mistrust but are in fact in cahoots with one another.

The league's head office is urging its thirty-two teams to take the muzzles off their players, but decades of conditioning are hard to change. Heidi Browning, the NHL's chief marketing officer, believes in the mantra "humans over highlights." Modern fans don't want to cheer on automatons. They want to know what makes the players tick.

Kim Davis, the NHL's executive vice president in charge of growth and diversity initiatives, says the dressing-room cultures of the member teams are both a blessing and a curse. She rightly points out that NHL players are approachable. I can vouch for the fact that they are generally polite and willing to answer questions. She notes how much players like to credit their teammates for their success. Ask Sidney Crosby about his

Stanley Cup rings, and I guarantee he'll immediately credit his teammates, coaches, and the fans who supported the Pittsburgh Penguins before talking about himself. Players regularly thank interviewers for taking the time to talk to them.

While the conversations are polite, the players are guarded. They are careful not to get too personal, too honest. They won't venture into the hot-button issues of the day. Davis wishes the players would be more, well, open. "But on the other side of that [being humble and approachable], can't you be that and have a point of view, too?" said Davis. "You can be all those things and, at the same time, be passionate about something, whatever that is. I think that's where we have to broaden our lens and our exposure, so we can understand that two things can be true at the same time."

That close-to-the-vest part of hockey culture has always been part of the game. When Willie O'Ree, the first Black player to skate in the NHL, was tapped to do his first interview on coast-to-coast television in Canada, he was asked about how tough it was to be hockey's answer to Jackie Robinson—he chose not to say anything about the time that fans in Chicoutimi, Quebec, tried to attack him in the penalty box. He didn't say anything about the racial barbs he heard on the ice. He simply said he heard "a few jeers," like every hockey player does.

That was more than six decades ago, but O'Ree stuck to the same code of "The Culture" that silently governs so many players today.

"You probably know what I mean by the 'hockey answer,'" O'Ree wrote in his autobiography.[4] "If you're looking for insight into deep questions, don't ask a hockey player with a mic in your hand and the cameras rolling. Hockey players tend to say as little as possible, because the less you say, the less you can say wrong."

But maybe I just perceive the players as not being outspoken, when in fact what they are is predictable. There are NHL players past and present who have spoken out on political issues, but the causes they support only amplify hockey as a haven for white conservatives. Hockey will not have players taking knees or raising their fists in the air when the national anthems are played. What it has offered is a series of mixed messages on issues of diversity and gay pride. When fans think of NHL players and political stances, they wouldn't be wrong if they think, "Can I take 'Conservative Politics of the 21st Century' for $800, Alex?"

Boston Bruins legend Bobby Orr publicly endorsed Donald Trump. Wayne Gretzky, the greatest player in the game, endorsed former Canadian Conservative prime minister Stephen Harper. On 2024's US election night, pictures snapped of Gretzky attending Donald Trump's victory party at Mar-a-Lago went viral. NHL defenseman Tony DeAngelo was vocal in his support of Trump, and NHL Hall of Famer and Chicago sports legend Chris Chelios endorsed Pat O'Brien, a Republican hang-'em-high, tough-on-crime candidate in the 2020 Cook County state's attorney election race. And in maybe hockey's most famous political stance to date, Boston Bruins goalie Tim Thomas blew off his team's post–Stanley Cup meet and greet with US president Barack Obama.

"I believe the federal government has grown out of control, threatening the rights, liberties, and property of the people," Thomas wrote on Facebook in 2012. "This is being done at the executive, legislative, and judicial level. This is in direct opposition to the constitution and the founding fathers' vision for the federal government.

"Because I believe this, today I exercised my right as a free citizen, and did not visit the White House. This was not about politics or party, as in my opinion both parties are responsible for the situation we are in as a country. This was about a choice I had to make as an individual."

Despite Thomas's social media posts, the optics of a white superstar refusing to have his picture taken with a Black president should have caused a large uproar. Instead, the controversy went away pretty quickly. The Bruins stated that the club did not consider Thomas's blowing off a team event a disciplinary issue.

Neither Orr, Gretzky, nor Thomas were really ever challenged by any major media figure in the hockey world to at least discuss their stances in an interview. Yet, when a Black NFL player, Colin Kaepernick, takes a knee during the national anthem, the media rush to say that since he was the one who brought up politics, it's fair game to criticize his politics.

When a hockey player retreats to politics of the (mostly) white and right, he gets a pass. The politics become a matter of personal choice, and after all, we should stick to sports.

Consider Alexander Ovechkin: we know in the hockey media that it's verboten to ask one of the greatest goal-scorers in NHL history about his support of Vladimir Putin. Even though he's made public shows of support for Russia's war effort in Ukraine, including Instagram posts with the hashtag #SaveChildrenFromFascism, he gets handled with kid gloves in North America. He launched Putin Team in 2017, to lend his massive celebrity within Russia to put even more gloss on his dear leader.

Too many within the hockey world fall back on the excuse that Ovechkin still has family in Russia, he has to toe the party line to keep them safe, he's in a bad spot. Sounds a bit like "we were just following orders," doesn't it?

Thomas and Ovechkin escape scrutiny. They are above reproach. Yet we wonder why hockey is perceived as a white man's game.

It's not like Ovechkin should be banned from hockey for having pro-Putin views. There are concepts of free speech, thought, and association that Canadians and Americans should hold dear. But if he puts his pro-Putin views out there for all to see, he shouldn't be allowed to use the hockey rink as a hiding place. He should answer questions about it.

THE ROOM

There's no doubt that hockey teams are close-knit groups. It's common practice in hockey for players to take the ice even if they're carrying severe injuries. When a team is eliminated from the playoffs, it's become a tradition that the general manager finally admits which players were nursing sprains, shoulder separations, and even bone breaks. Players will sprawl in front of pucks being shot at them at over ninety miles per hour. They will step in when a teammate falls victim to a hit they feel crosses the line.

But they will also go out of their way not to rock the boat—and it's led to a culture where even sexual assaults, like the 2010 Blackhawks cover-up of the assault on Kyle Beach, to the 2018 investigations into the allegations of the 2018 Canadian junior national team's group assault of a woman in a hotel in London, Ontario, haven't come to the surface until years later.

And the codes we see in dressing rooms—whether they be at the NHL level or in a small-town rink—have been set by white team captains and white coaches. These traditions have been passed down throughout the years. The dressing room "code" is entirely a white construct.

As Robin DiAngelo writes in *White Fragility: Why It's So Hard for White People to Talk About Racism*, the idea of "respect" in society has been created by whites. And that is true of the power structures within hockey teams. "What feels respectful to white people can be exactly what does not create a respectful environment for people of color. For example, white people often define as respectful an environment with no conflict, no expression of strong emotion, no challenging of racist patterns, and a focus on intentions over impact. But such an atmosphere is exactly what creates an inauthentic, white-norm-centered, and thus hostile environment for people of color."[5]

Think of this in terms of what happened to Akim Aliu in Rockford. He felt powerless to speak out against his coach's racial epithets. He felt he would be breaking that code if he was to go public, that his career would be ruined. And he wasn't wrong. If a player speaks out against the team's culture, he's likely to be the one branded as the bad apple. The overwhelming power of hockey's dressing room culture has allowed too much injustice to pass by.

In the media, there are a few exceptions—there are still some of us who will ask a tough question or understand that sports should be a doorway to ask some deeper, societal questions (think of Rick Westhead and the investigative work he has done for TSN in Canada). But far too many of us wearing lanyards are quite content not to delve deeply into issues other than why a team's special teams are struggling or why a goaltender is struggling. The rise of analytics in sports has given the media a shiny new toy, and we often write stories that read more like grade-11 math problems than narratives about anything of real importance.

We don't ask questions about why NHL owners donate money to Republican campaigns at a seven-to-one ratio over Democratic campaigns.[6] We don't ask why Colorado Avalanche owner Stan Kroenke made a seven-figure donation to Donald Trump's inauguration campaign,[7] or why Oilers owner Daryl Katz has invested in Laura Ingraham's right-wing "news" site, *LifeZette*.[8] NHL teams have a rocky record when it comes to support of Pride initiatives and, again, aren't really taken to task by the media who cover them. Race is an issue that's rarely discussed in press boxes.

As well, there are a number of online media pundits who serve as armchair critics, who criticize players but don't go into the dressing rooms to look said players and coaches in the eye.

Media is shrinking, there is no doubt about that. I'm accredited to cover the Edmonton Oilers, and, while at about 1.5 million, the city's metro area is small compared with many other NHL cities, in hockey circles, it is a major team. It is a team that commands its market and is easily the number one game in town. *Forbes* valued the Oilers at $1.85 billion USD at the end of 2023, seventh of the thirty-two teams.

The team moved into shiny $613.7 million CAD Rogers Place in 2016, and with it came a two-tiered press box with seating for more than a hundred media and VIPs. It is rarely close to half-full. Many nights, I am surrounded by empty seats, while the arena below is full.

The media who do survive deal with tight deadlines and the demand to write more stories. The workloads have increased, as one journalist is expected to do the work that three journalists did a decade ago.

As the media availabilities go by quickly, we often divvy up the work. One group will go to the Oilers room, the other goes to the visiting team's room—at the other side of the arena—and then we reconvene and pool resources. That is, we each transcribe a certain player's or coach's quotes and we share them. There is no big ethical quandary here because, heck, the team's social media account is going to stream these availabilities, anyway, and these scrums are going to be on the team's website ASAP. There is no exclusivity.

So, with those pressures, it's become a race to the bottom. Deep down, we're fully aware that if we take a knife to the sport we care about so much, it could be our jobs that become victims to it all. It's a vicious cycle.

What has been created is an space of total media safety, and we have become the worst censors of all—self-censors.

As I read Howard Bryant's essay on how he saw his ESPN colleagues shun the social challenges that came with Colin Kaepernick's decision to kneel through "The Star Spangled Banner," something clicked with me. Because, in a lot of ways, what Bryant wrote could also be applied to how hockey journalists have shied away from the Russia-Ukraine war, from race, and from Pride.

Bryant wrote that journalists understand what kind of stories tick off the team owners and league head offices, and will naturally shy away from them. "Corporations rely on employees self-censoring to ensure that trouble for its business relationships is kept at a minimum. Pretty much everyone working at any corporation knows where they stand upon entering the building."[9]

In an era when we're all wondering if this is the morning that will bring the pink slip, the motivation to stick a neck out isn't just reduced, it's eliminated. Yes, there was a blip in 2020, when the NHL playoffs were held in the bubble. Matt Dumba took to the mic and called for change in the game of hockey. Ryan Reaves, then a player with the Vegas Golden Knights, led a movement to have two days' worth of playoff games postponed, in protest of the police shooting of Jacob Blake.

But when it came to reacting to the Blake shooting, the NHL took its sweet time. The boycotting of games was something NBA and MLB players had already done, so, in terms of sticking their necks out as a collective, this was a low-risk proposal for NHLers. In fact, a cynic would say the NHL Players' Association was late to the party, and only acted after seeing public support for the stances already taken by pro baseball and basketball players. Pierre-Edouard Bellemare, a Black NHLer who played for the Colorado Avalanche at the time, said that it took NHLers too long to make their public stand on the shooting of Blake. "It didn't feel right," he said of the players' sluggish response.[10] "After reflecting on it and us being here together [in the bubble], it's the best response we could have."

But at least for a few weeks, hockey's politics weren't white and right, or at least someone had changed the window dressing.

Something I see a lot in sports journalism are writers and broadcasters congratulating themselves for asking the hard questions. Asking the superstar forward why he's in a scoring slump. Walking into the dressing room of a team on a five-game losing streak, where players utter one-word answers to questions without making eye contact with the cameras.

The thing is, these aren't hard questions at all. It's all part and parcel of the game within the game—the relationship between the teams and the media. Even at their surliest, the players have to come out and talk to the press. And the questions stay within the realm of what happened on the ice, or what can be expected on the next road trip. There's an unwritten concord at play; and, soon, the dressing room visits blend into a routine, and the only reason we're standing there with the recording devices on is to prove that we were there.

The press huddles are so safe, the teams' own communications staffs have no issue showing them live on their websites and social media feeds. They are that certain that no one will ask about social issues or how the game fits into a wider societal context.

Davis has said repeatedly that the NHL invites interrogation. But who is out there, willing to ask the hard questions? And so, the more things change, the more they stay the same.

EIGHT

WHERE WILL WE BE A CENTURY FROM NOW?

I SIT WITH LALI Toor in the lounge of a downtown Edmonton hotel. There are hockey highlights playing on the many television screens that surround us.

Toor's words hang in the air: Will hockey survive the next one hundred years? In the twenty-second century, will the game be a major part of the North American sports landscape, will it be relegated to an extreme niche sport, or will all the hockey arenas have been converted to pickleball courts?

It seems absurd. We are in a hotel that was constructed next to an NHL arena as part of a downtown revitalization project. You can't avoid Oilers logos in any direction that you look. But despite where we are at that moment, Toor's question has a lot of merit. And it's not an easy one to answer.

Understand that Toor is not a casual observer. In 2017, he founded Apna Hockey, a program that introduces kids of color to the game, with an emphasis on Indo-Canadians and Indo-Americans. The movement was later joined by Dampy Brar, a Calgarian who played minor pro hockey in places like Las Vegas, Tacoma, San Antonio, and Nashville. In 2021, they won the NHL's Willie O'Ree Community Hero Award, for their work in promoting diversity in hockey.

While Apna Hockey has made some inroads, including a formal partnership with the Winnipeg Jets that was announced at the team's South

Asian Heritage Night in December of 2023, Toor is frustrated by how slow the change of pace has been in hockey.

"Change is not a bottom-up process," says Toor. "It's never been a bottom-up process. There's a bunch of white owners at the top. And do they care about growing the game? The game of hockey never grew. The culture suffocated its own game. We have a bunch of Caucasian CEOs and executives who don't understand how to collaborate."

Toor likens the progress in hockey to how slow it was for O'Ree to finally be recognized by the NHL for his trailblazing role in the game. "I always run up against the culture," says Lali, who said we all need to remember that the O'Ree Award is named for a player who really only got the chance to play a handful of games in the NHL. "Although we have opened doors with Apna Hockey with the O'Ree Trophy, and we've had some real positive outcomes, sometimes it still feels we're as mistreated as Willie was back in the day."

Toor and Brar were running camps for six years, with the moral support of NHL teams—stress moral support—until the Jets became the first team to develop a true financial partnership with the charity. That was followed by a $30,000 donation from the Calgary Flames in 2024. "It feels like, for the first time in six years, there's a team that understands what we are trying to do with this," he says. "When new families move to Winnipeg, they want to capture those families."

But he believes that a program run by South Asian Canadians, aimed at North American kids who come from South Asian backgrounds, is a story that's too good to be true for NHL front offices, which are mainly white. "It's like, despite what we've done, they don't trust us," he says. "We still have to show our worth. How many times do we have to show our worth? What does the Willie O'Ree Award even mean? It's not a question for us to answer. It's a question for the teams in the league to answer. I thought it was going to open doors for us, where we would become accepted and collaborate."

When Toor tells his life story, it's easy to understand his impatience with the game. But it might be even easier to ask yourself, how can a person love the game so much that he tries and tries to rebuild the culture, even though he was rejected over and over by the sport?

Let's go back in time.

Toor felt the sting of racism in hockey. He was a promising young player in the Edmonton area but thought that he was denied opportunities to excel in AAA hockey. By the time he was in his late teens, he wasn't playing anymore. Like many racialized kids, the barriers were too big to overcome. But instead of growing bitter and forgetting about hockey, he made it his mission to change the game.

Apna translates to "our" hockey from the Punjabi language. "That word meant so much to me growing up," said Toor. "Because, growing up, I never saw our people at the rink." What Toor wants is for kids growing up to have something he never had—mentorship and support.

Toor's dad came to Canada from India in the 1980s. At the time, Wayne Gretzky and the Edmonton Oilers were changing the way hockey was played. This was the team that the NHL, as part of its one hundredth anniversary celebrations, recognized as its greatest team of all time. Toor's dad fell in love with hockey, and it was a love he passed down to his son. Toor embraced the game. He could skate like the wind. He was being picked for top-level rep teams. He played in rep programs with future NHLers Brendan Gallagher and Colton Parayko. But there were roadblocks everywhere. "It exists overtly, but even worse is the systemic racism," says Lali. "It really hurt me. It got to the point where other parents felt bad about it. They'd tell my dad that his son was a wicked player, but it won't be an easy road."

His family switched him from one minor-hockey organization to the next, but the same issues were there. Toor remembers being cut from an AAA team and being replaced by a player who was injured. The team chose a player who could not play over him. In his second year of eligibility, that same coach called him upstairs and told him that he was one of the last players to make the team, and that he should feel lucky to have gotten that chance.

When he was ten years old, he was simply asked to leave a minor-hockey league team in the suburban community of St. Albert.

"It got so toxic, that I was kicked off a team halfway through the season," says Toor. He said that parents complained that he wasn't eligible to be on the Atom team, even though he was approved by the minor-hockey association at the start of the season.

Toor was frustrated, and he sought out advice from a former NHL player. "He told me that God has given you this gift, you skate like the wind. But it's not going to be an easy road. This is white man's sport. It's not meant for ethnic minorities."

Now, Apna Hockey is designed to open doors and break barriers. There are hockey camps for kids, supported by the Oilers and Flames. There were discussions with the Dallas Stars about holding camps there, but Lali believes that kids in nontraditional hockey cities, places where ice isn't readily accessible, should be first introduced to the game through ball hockey. Apna has also had talks with the Los Angeles Kings about holding camps in Southern California. "It's giving a community that genuinely loves hockey the glue," said Lali. "We're a network. It's turned into everything I never had growing up. I never had mentors growing up."

There are challenges. Despite Kim Davis's strong words about trying to convey a strong diversity message through all thirty-two of its teams, Toor sees a league where there is little collaboration between the clubs. When he pitches Apna Hockey as a potential partner, he has to visit each club independently—there's no central channel for him to approach the league and have his message funnel to thirty-two different front offices.

And there's the big thing. As the season progresses, coaches see outreach programs as unnecessary distractions for their players. Note that most teams hold their hospital visits and charity drives early in the season. As we get closer to playoff time, the public appearances stop.

Toor says what the old-guard, hockey-was-always-played-this-way doesn't see is how the lack of outreach hurts the game. In the end, he says some teams will have to make a hard decision—"What's more important? Winning a Cup or growing the game?" Or, better yet, is there a way to do both?

So, how does hockey change?

Apna Hockey is working with NHL teams to create more opportunities for minority players. But Toor says, no matter what is said, no matter how many programs are created, change won't come until there are BIPOC owners of NHL teams. As Toor points out, not one of the thirty-two NHL teams has a person of color as a majority owner.

In 2022, Mike Grier became the first Black general manager in NHL history, taking over the reins of the San Jose Sharks. Xavier A. Gutierrez, who was the president of the Arizona Coyotes before the team was sold and relocated to Salt Lake City ahead of the 2024–25 season, was the first-ever

Latino to hold that high a position in an NHL front office. Jarome Iginla is special adviser to Calgary Flames general manager Craig Conroy. But these are small first steps.

Davis said that the NHL has to understand that BIPOC communities are filled with "fans-in-waiting" and that they represent "the future of the sport." Davis is in an unusual position in the NHL. The owners are all white men. The commissioner is a white man, as is the league's top legal counsel.

As DiAngelo notes in *White Fragility*, "White implicit bias is always at play because all humans have bias, inequity can occur simply through homogeneity; if I am not aware of the barriers you face, then I won't see them, much less be motivated to remove them."[1] I'd take this train of thought even further: many of these white institutions will pause and recognize inequities, but then struggle to solve them. Attempts by the NHL to have Pride Nights, to hold Hockey Is for Everyone events, they're well meaning, but they can fall flat because, at the head, they're designed by white people who see the inequities through their lenses. Rather than turn over the keys, they're still driving the car. Inequities aren't always ignored, but those of us coming from positions of wealth and whiteness (those who own NHL teams) are not naturally equipped to be the change agents the game needs.

While it's certainly promoted as a noble enterprise, Hockey Is for Everyone has its critics. Courtney Szto has been cited quite a bit in this book, and she warns that, while it is a feel-good enterprise, these programs also normalize the idea that hockey is white centered. The game is for everyone, finally—after whites open the door. It suggests that players of color are being permitted to play.

"HIFE coincides with Black History Month, and, much like Black history, is necessary because every other month inherently leaves white supremacy unmarked," Szto writes in *Changing on the Fly*.[2] "It is the one month where pointing out difference is acceptable, so long as there is a positive story attached. What is often lost in these displays of shallow multiculturalism is that the celebration of culture and difference simultaneously protects the white privilege that takes place on the ice."

The owners are the ones who make money off hockey. They are the ones who reap the benefits of the television deals, ticket sales, and sponsorships.

Some of the oldest NHL teams are family businesses, passed down from one generation to the next, or are owned by even larger companies. And the values of NHL teams are skyrocketing. *Forbes* magazine annually appraises the values of NHL teams. In the 2021 ranking, nine teams were worth more than $1 billion USD. Twenty-five were worth more than $600 million USD. It's a massive investment to take on, and teams don't get put up for sale very often.

In 2023, there was a chance for that status quo to change, just a little bit. In the sports world, we see more and more celebrities who are part of sports ownership teams. While actor Ryan Reynolds has transformed his co-ownership of lower-tier British soccer team Wrexham into a smash-hit reality TV series, his heavy stake in the team is unusual for the Hollywood types. Typically, the celebrity is brought in as a minority stakeholder by the much wealthier power brokers to be the "face" of the deal. While pop stars, actors, and professional athletes have millions of dollars at their disposal, they don't have the hundreds of millions or even billions of dollars in capital needed to buy big-time sports teams. That's left to the real estate, stock market, and health care magnates, the hedge funds, the Russian oligarchs (before the war in Ukraine, at least), and the oil wealth of the Middle East.

But after the death of Ottawa Senators owner Eugene Melnyk, the team was put up for sale. Reynolds threw in with one group vying to buy the team, but the presence of two Black pop-music stars, one American, one Canadian, in rival bids was new ground for a league where the faces in the Board of Governors meetings are all white.

Snoop Dogg was part of a Los Angeles–based bid led by Neko Sparks; Abel Tesfaye, known by his stage name, The Weeknd, was part of a bid led by Canadian billionaires Jeffrey and Michael Kimel. They eventually lost out to a group led by Michael Andlauer, a Canadian transportation baron.

Snoop Dogg's cult of personality took over the Sparks bid, and that wasn't a bad thing. He took to Instagram to tell fans of the Senators that the Sparks group wanted to reach out to Indigenous groups in Canada, to see if they'd want to buy shares in the team. "We're trying to do something, we're trying to make a difference," said the rapper, wearing a black Senators jersey. "I mean, it's all official like a referee with a whistle. We're all together, we're trying to make it better, we just need you all to hit the lever and give us control." He said that he cherishes a jersey that was given to him by Ray Emery in 2007, before the Senators faced the Anaheim Ducks in the Stanley Cup final.[3]

Had the NHL gotten a celebrity of color like Snoop Dogg into the ownership fold, even as a minority face in a larger investment group, it would have helped slow, or possibly stop, a pop-culture trend that hockey is white. Yes, there are NHL clubs that have minority owners of color; but these are quiet, behind-the-scenes voices. Snoop would have been a larger-than-life presence. When it comes to those who have the votes at Board of Governors meetings, that's still 100 percent the domain of whites.

Now it's Anson Carter, who appears prominently in this book, who looks to be the celebrity lead of a new ownership group. In March of 2024, Carter announced he's a partner in Alpharetta Sports & Entertainment Group, which looks to bring an expansion team to Atlanta. Carter and his group hope that the third time is the charm for NHL hockey in Georgia, as two teams have failed there before—the Atlanta Flames relocated to Calgary, and the Atlanta Thrashers became the Winnipeg Jets 2.0.

WHEN HOCKEY HAD POP-CULTURE POWER

Go back to the late 1980s: Wayne Gretzky, arguably the best player in a team sport who ever lived (I'm Canadian, so you should quickly be able to place my bias on the whole Jordan/Pele/Messi/Gretzky/LeBron debate), has been traded by the Edmonton Oilers to the Los Angeles Kings, part of a deal that would help cash-strapped Oilers owner Peter Pocklington shed salary.

The boost to hockey as a whole in North America was astounding. The Los Angeles Kings changed their team colors to black and silver, and, heck, people even started to see replica jerseys in rap videos. NWA did a photo shoot with members in Kings caps. Black and silver? Gretzky? Hockey had gone from clear No. 4 sport in the United States…to cool. Gretzky would host *Saturday Night Live* in 1989, joining a rare athletes' pantheon usually reserved for Super Bowl champs.

In 1998, Spike Lee directed ads promoting the NHL playoffs, with legendary comedian Flip Wilson portraying a preacher who extols the virtues of the game. But in modern times, hockey is often parodied as being too white, too Canadian, for mainstream America. The irony is that the percentage of Canadian players has fallen, and there are a number of teams in the league that have more Americans under contract than they do Canadians.

In 2016, *Saturday Night Live* welcomed Canadian rap icon Drake onto the stage as both host and musical guest. The most memorable skit of the night was when he played "Jared," a Canadian guesting on "Black Jeopardy!" When Drake picks the "Bruh…" category, Kenan Thompson asks the contestants to name an athlete who's been playing for a long time, and still putting up "big numbers." Drake answers with…Jaromir Jagr.

"Jaromir say what now?" Thompson shoots back with big laughs from the studio audience. "Jared, I know you're speaking English, but it ain't my English."

Chance the Rapper appeared on *SNL* in 2017. In one skit, he played a sports broadcaster who normally covers the Knicks but has to fill in as the Rangers game-day reporter. He is asked to describe the game. "Lots of white dudes on skates, running into each other at full speed. I do not get it." Again, big laughs, and the Rangers reacted by having their in-house video team ask their players what they thought of the skit. Their responses made for a collection of *aw shucks, it was cool* video snippets.

But the message was there. The premise of a celebrity of color in a hockey environment makes for a memorable comedy skit. The idea of hip-hop culture coming anywhere near hockey is the stuff that makes for absurdist viewing. And the chance of the NHL's biggest stars being asked to host *Saturday Night Live* in the modern era? Nil—even though the man behind the show, Lorne Michaels, is Canadian.

This is where Davis's mission statement, that the NHL has to reach potential new fans, has to ring true. Because we've already seen that when players of color are placed in the spotlight, the positive reaction far outweighs what the trolls post online.

The Jets' celebration of South Asian heritage was not the team's first foray into multicultural outreach. In October of 2022, hockey fans in Winnipeg saw change in action. The team celebrated Filipino Heritage Night, and the Jets skated out for their pregame warm-up in jerseys that had red, blue, and gold elements from the flag of that Asian nation. The irony is that the Jets had no players of Filipino heritage on their roster. But the visiting team from Dallas did.

Jason Robertson is the second player of Filipino heritage to skate in the NHL, and the Dallas Stars forward has emerged as a bona fide superstar. He scored 41 goals in 2021–22, and continued that torrid pace into the 22–23 season. He finished the season with 109 points, sixth in the league. He became the first Stars player to have a 100-point season since the team moved from Minnesota to Dallas back in 1993. Dallas won the Stanley Cup in 1999, lost in the finals in 2000 and 2020, and have had Hall of Famers Brett Hull and Mike Modano skate for them. But neither of those players put together a season like Robertson did in 2022–23.

Robertson fully understands what it means to be an Asian American star in the NHL. Robertson was born and raised in California, and then played junior hockey with the Kingston Frontenacs of the Ontario Hockey League before he was drafted by the Stars. "It's definitely great to be a role model," he said the night before the Stars took the ice in Winnipeg. "The next game we'll play is Filipino Heritage night, and that's definitely something that's kinda cool and special."

It was no accident that the Jets scheduled that event for when Robertson and the Stars were coming to town. Robertson's emergence as an NHL star even has opposing teams programming special events around him. "I'm just trying to be a good idol," said Robertson, whose brother, Nick, plays for the Maple Leafs. "I know that people come up to me, and it's great. I try to present myself as a great professional on the ice and off the ice. If I can be a role model for those kids [of color] it's definitely exciting, and I embrace that."

Most of the Canadian teams have land acknowledgments before their home games, before the national anthems. The acknowledgment is a way of publicly honoring the treaties made with Indigenous nations. Many of the arenas sit on treaty land.

Even though NHL headquarters made an edict in 2023 that themed cultural jerseys could not be worn during warm-ups, a response to the Pride controversy I've covered earlier in this book, teams are still seeing the value of making and selling these themed shirts. There's the outreach portion—and then it goes back to what Davis said about seeing diversity as a business decision. If a team makes a cool-looking Black History Month, Indigenous-themed, or Lunar New Year jersey, there are fan bases out there looking to buy them.

When the NHL announced the jersey restrictions, the Edmonton Oilers didn't abandon their plans to celebrate Pride, Indigenous heritage, the South Asian Community, Lunar New Year, or Black History Month. Plans remained in place to feature those jerseys in other ways, even if no Oiler could wear them on the ice.

"We can spotlight the communities that are such an important part of our fanbase," said Dan Cote-Rosen, the Oilers Entertainment Group's vice president of marketing. "What we can offer these communities is our platform, but we feel the power of our platform is significant."

The team reached out to local street artist AJA Louden to design the Black History Month logo, which was based on African weaving traditions. Sunny Nerval drew a bright peacock to celebrate South Asian heritage. Vietnamese Canadian artist Pete Nguyen designed a logo that celebrated the Year of the Dragon. "This wasn't a case of someone telling me they wanted to do something a certain way," Nguyen said. "They really leaned on me. The symbolism was on me to build."

Indigenous artist Lance Cardinal's turtle logo is where it all began. North America is referred to as "Turtle Island" in several Indigenous languages—and Cardinal's logo was a reminder that we live on settled land, with many acts of reconciliation still needing to be done.

In an earlier chapter, I wrote about how the historical framing of the American Revolution and the War of 1812 acts as a barrier to celebrating the Colored Hockey League. In Canada, we are early in reconciliation, but this is a challenge that our American neighbors have yet to take on. Imagine the Kansas City Chiefs or Atlanta Braves or Chicago Blackhawks asking artists from local Indigenous nations to design logos for them, rather than use the ones white artists and marketing departments created. If these teams aren't going to change their names or stop the painful practices of war drums and tomahawk chops, the least they could do is allow Indigenous people to define how they want to be seen.

OK, I need to step down from the soapbox and get back to the matter at hand—why outreach matters. Here's more proof. In chapter 3, I wrote about Arshdeep Bains, the Punjabi Canadian kid from Surrey, BC, who was signed by the Vancouver Canucks after he led the Western Hockey League in scoring.

Bains's progress is enthusiastically followed in Greater Vancouver. According to the 2021 Canadian census, more than 180,000 residents in Vancouver and the surrounding suburbs stated that they could speak Punjabi. The potential market for a hockey star of Indian descent is massive. It's just that the hockey world hasn't quite realized it yet.

The Bains story is a compelling one. He wasn't drafted, but he didn't give up his dream. He knew his junior team, the Red Deer Rebels, had produced undrafted players who had made it in the NHL, like Reese Johnson of the Chicago Blackhawks and Brandon Hagel of the Tampa Bay Lightning. And then a dream came true; not only was he offered a deal by an NHL team, but it came from the Canucks.

"A lot of things come into play," said Bains. "I thought I was playing better every year. And there's a good coaching system in Red Deer, developing the players, a lot of players there have been able to sign as twenty-year-olds, and that's a sign of how good the Red Deer Rebels are at developing players. I saw athletes before me, like Hagel and Johnson, getting contracts when they are twenty, and I thought, why can't I do that? I came into the year with confidence, and I was able to get myself a contract, as well.

"The Canucks were definitely the first team to offer, and I took it right away. There was a lot going on in the mix, with teams interested in me. But the first *offer* came from the Canucks, and I couldn't say no to the hometown team. That was the team I wanted, and I think if any other team offered, I still would have chosen Vancouver."

After he signed with the Canucks in 2022, Bains participated in a Hockey Is for Everyone event in Surrey, BC. Even though he was just starting to make his way in the Canucks organization, Bains knew many Indo-Canadian kids are already looking up to him.

"I think most guys are role models when they come into professional hockey," said Arshdeep. "I don't know how many [Indian players] there are right now, but there are a few. But people do look up to me, and I can't let them down, I can't have any slipups. There's pros and cons to it, but if you can be a role model, there's lots you can do in this game.

"When I was sixteen and I first played in the Western League, people would tell me, 'Congrats, this is really big.' As soon as I signed with Vancouver, it was completely different. There were a lot of people reaching out. And even people who didn't know me weren't afraid to come up to me. Even when I was getting my skates sharpened in the summer, kids would come up to me because they recognized me. It's a privilege that I get looked up to. You're not going to make it in one season, it's a long journey. So, for people to look up to me, I am honored, but it's not something that goes to my head. It helps push me."

When Bains made his NHL debut, before he got onto the ice, he was filmed performing a *maatha taek*, a Sikh religious gesture of deference. As he was in the hallway leading from the dressing room to the ice, he reached down and touched the ground. He was wearing his Canucks jersey, but honored his faith.

That clip was posted on Apna Hockey's Instagram page and got hundreds of thousands of views.

Bains said the pushes from the grassroots show that hockey is slowly becoming more welcoming. And he said if different, racialized groups can be brought together to celebrate the game, it would help hockey as a whole.

"It's been heading in the right direction. I think that, twenty years ago, it wasn't like it is now, I'd bet. If a player like [Jason] Robertson could run a camp for Filipinos, and we can have a camp for Indians, it would make the game better. It doesn't have to be super serious and competitive. Just have people come out, with sticks and skates and whatever you need. But obviously, it has to be free. It's an expensive sport. And if we want to bring diversity into the game, we have to understand that there's people out there who can't afford it."

In 2020, while he was still a member of the Minnesota Wild, defenseman Matt Dumba was named as the recipient of that year's King Clancy Award. The prize, which comes from the NHL, is given "to the player who best exemplifies leadership qualities on and off the ice and has made a noteworthy humanitarian contribution in his community."

In his time with the Wild, Dumba was a big supporter of ACES. It's a program in the Twin Cities of Minneapolis and St. Paul that uses examples from sports to help kids in grades 4–8 to stay engaged in their schoolwork. There's an understanding that sport can help kids from marginalized communities do better in school and want to be more engaged in their classrooms. It's supported by all the major league teams in the area—and the University of Minnesota, too.

"It provides a safe haven for kids after school, where they can get additional help and do that through learning with sports," said Dumba. "It keeps them engaged, and it gives them the chance to further themselves and learn something new. I've been with ACES since the start of my career, and I've seen so many kids who have been helped along the way. I am very proud of that, and they do a great job over there."

The Vegas Golden Knights is a young franchise, less than a decade old, but has already won a Cup—and Zach Whitecloud, the Dakota Sioux defenseman, helps with the team's outreach programs. Located in the desert, Las Vegas doesn't get snow or cold weather. According to the US Census numbers from 2022, it is a diverse city, with only 55 percent of the population identifying itself as "white only." Whitecloud said that bringing the diverse Vegas population to hockey as a spectator sport is one thing, but it takes more to introduce them to the game as a participation sport.

"The way hockey is going, and it's not just about my background specifically, it's become a sport that's become tough to access," said Zach. "Obviously, first and foremost, if you live in a place where there isn't a ton of snow and the temperature isn't favorable for outdoor rinks, the only access people have is indoor ice. And the costs to rent ice have gone through the roof. In terms of making hockey more inclusive, floor hockey, outdoor hockey, street hockey, those sorts of things allow people to grow their love for the game and see if they have a passion for it. Down here in Vegas, we have outdoor clinics every now and again. Through the team, there's been street hockey and ways to make hockey more accessible, specifically for Las Vegas. But I think it could be the same back home [in Manitoba], too."

The team has not only held street hockey clinics in Vegas but has brought ball hockey to school gyms in different parts of Nevada. This is how hockey is built; before a family has to decide whether to become invested in skates and pads and all the expenses that come with ice time, they can first experience the game on the hard court or the street.

According to numbers provided by the NHL, the number of registered hockey players in Nevada has grown by 268 percent since the

Knights entered the league as an expansion franchise back in 2017. The NHL and NHLPA have invested $3.6 million since that time to grow the game in an area of the United States that has never been tradition-ally associated with hockey. In late June of 2024, Whitecloud joined with Knights alumni and other members of the NHL's Player Inclusion Coalition to shepherd Las Vegas and area kids through on-ice and ball hockey clinics.

These are all examples of pro players of color doing their little parts when it comes to outreach. In Crystal M. Fleming's *How to Be Less Stupid About Race*, the American sociologist writes about how fighting structural racism is a slow process. To steal a coaching cliché, we have to "be in it, to win it." If we could all do what we can within our spheres of interest or influence, we can move that needle ever so slightly. Change comes from a lot of small, deliberate actions. These players are doing their bits to push that needle.

So, the outreach work from players of color helps, but alone it won't ensure that hockey is a going concern one hundred years from now. We also need massive changes in the grassroots.

FROM THE GROUND UP

When it comes to hockey, Irfan Chaudhry's got a big job ahead of him. As the vice president of diversity and inclusion at Hockey Canada, he is in charge of creating diversity initiatives for an organization that not only is facing shrinking registration numbers but has been rocked by scandal. Sponsors have withdrawn support. The federal government sus-pended funding to the organization. The spotlight was thrust on Hockey Canada when an alleged 2018 incident came to light. Five members of the gold-medal-winning Canadian junior hockey team were accused of sexually assaulting a woman after a team function in London, Ontario. Through government inquiry into the incident, it was discovered that Hockey Canada had a slush fund, funded by taxpayers and registration fees, to pay off sexual assault victims.

Reports have been written. Hugh Fraser took over as the first Black board chair in Hockey Canada's history. (He has since stepped down.) In 2024, five players were formally charged in relation to the incident in

London, Ontario: Philadelphia Flyers goalie Carter Hart, New Jersey Devils teammates Cal Foote and Michael McLeod, Dillon Dube of the Calgary Flames, and former Ottawa Senator Alex Formenton.

As well, the Canadian Hockey League, which oversees the three major junior leagues in North America, is still fighting a nearly decade-old class action lawsuit from former players, who alleged they were permanently affected by a culture of hazing, abuse, and discrimination. In 2020, an independent panel found that abuse is so prevalent in the CHL, it's become a "cultural norm."

Chaudhry knows that his appointment was not because of a need to be progressive, but because Canadian hockey has been rocked by scandal, and the powers that be have to show that they are doing *something, anything*.

"It's unfortunate that it took something like this to be a wake-up call," Chaudhry said.

But even though it took a crisis and a Chernobyl amount of fallout for Hockey Canada to finally make diversity and inclusion a priority, the key is to look forward. What has to change?

"We have to be intentional about growth and retention, and understand that the bread and butter will always be there," said Chaudhry. The bread and butter are middle-class-to-wealthy white families.

"On a national level, how do we ensure broader participation and retention?"

Chaudhry said the key is data. Numbers are important. Hockey Canada has launched a passport program, which tracks the racial backgrounds of players registered in the system. It's one thing to track the races, genders, and ages of the kids who are signing up to play the game, but it's more important to track when and where players are quitting. For example, if there's a trend of female Indigenous tweens quitting in and around Vancouver, Hockey Canada can react. The organization can ask questions about why these players are leaving at a certain age, and then create programming that might stop the player bleed.

He said that the people who run hockey, from the offices of Hockey Canada to the minor-hockey-association presidents from the Atlantic to the Arctic to the Pacific, have to accept that systemic and institutional bias exist, and have to be willing to ask themselves this hard question: "Who is included and who is excluded?"

Chaudhry understands that most people in hockey say the right thing. But people of color are used to well-meaning platitudes, a lot of white self-congratulation, then a total lack of follow-through. "It's about engaging on the path forward. Many organizations make diversity plans and then don't do anything after that."

The white majority needs to better understand the subtleties of race—when a player introduces a characteristic that's not evident in the majority, it needs to be met with acceptance. If a player has a Black History Month pin on his or her hockey bag, or wears a religious symbol that's not a cross, does it make the majority uncomfortable? And how does the white majority welcome that into the dressing room?

Chaudhry knows that most people who coach kids, who fill the water bottles and book the hotel rooms for the road trips, are volunteers. There are some mandatory online coaching modules that coaches and officials need to complete, but it's not the race training that's needed, and was championed by Matt Dumba way back in chapter 3. These volunteers take most of their cues from the National Hockey League. They see it as the ideal.

And Chaudhry said that the league has given off a series of mixed messages when it comes to race. It's not quite yet the North Star that Kim Davis hopes it will become. In 2023, the NHL banned Pride jerseys and anything that could be considered politically loaded from being worn on the ice; but as the Israel-Palestine conflict erupted, the Edmonton Oilers had "Stand With Israel" messaging as part of a pregame ceremony. The NHL and NHLPA issued a joint statement condemning terrorism and the "loss of life in Israel." The league had issued a mandate to its teams to be apolitical, at least when it came to their forward faces, but then didn't follow its own rule.

As well, the league's brass wants to see the players be more open with the media and the public, to let their personalities shine through—and break through the culture. The fact that there are so many mixed messages is probably proof that what Toor has said about the NHL needing more unified, direct messaging from the top is probably true. This is a league that is still trying to find its way and be the role model at the same time.

"We have a directive from the league that restricts the promotion of certain causes, such as Pride Tape, but that same week we had teams take strong stances on the Israel-Gaza conflict," said Chaudhry. "We need to understand there are different identifications in the game.

"We have to understand media frames our understanding of sport, and many hockey officials are volunteers who get much of their information about hockey from media, and it shapes their unconscious bias they bring to the ice. If it's not backed up with education, the unconscious bias sets in."

While Chaudhry is a leading agent for change in the game, and has allies, there are still roadblocks. Soon after I spoke to Chaudhry for this book, the president of Hockey Quebec, former NHL goalie Jocelyn Thibault, announced that he would be stepping down.

When he took the job in 2021, Thibault pledged to tackle the province's culture, from parental harassment of coaches and referees to making the game more equitable. When he quit less than three years later, he cited a "resistance to change" in the province's grassroots culture.

For USA Hockey's Stephanie Jackson, it's about how people of color, people from marginalized groups, queer people, see the hockey rink in the years to come. "The biggest takeaway for the US market, despite everything that is said, every colloquialism, every bit of academia, about inclusion and diversity efforts, it doesn't mean anything if people don't feel that they can not only come in, but thrive, in our space."

Jackson said that USA Hockey is going through a "360-degree process" when it comes to cultural competency and awareness. Executives at USA Hockey and members of their affiliate groups are being asked to ask themselves to reflect on what it's like to be the "other" in a community filled with white parents, coaches, and kids.

In 2021, USA Hockey began a series of annual meetings with presidents of its thirty-seven affiliate organizations, to learn about and then discuss "how USA Hockey is perceived in different communities," according to Jackson. They discuss how hockey can do better when it comes to inclusivity, what partnerships can be sought out, where money needs to be spent—and where money *shouldn't* be spent.

A Hockey Network Scholarship was also created, where two Americans from diverse backgrounds are sent to one of the biggest annual conferences in the hockey industry—the North American Rink and Conference Expo. It's a conference about not just the sport itself but the business behind the game. That's because diversity is more than just seeing players of color on the ice; it's about having people of color be on the boards of associations, to manage the rinks, to work in the offices of amateur and professional clubs.

"We have found that the reason that hockey feels exclusionary is because diverse people are not in the room where things happen," said Jackson.

As well, affiliates who receive grant blocks from USA Hockey are now required to spend 15 percent of that money on diversity initiatives, whether it be modules to educate coaches, or reserving ice times where diverse athletes can come down to the rink.

The biggest enemy for diversity in hockey? According to Jackson, it's the status quo. For generations, local hockey associations have survived through connections and word of mouth. Does a minor-hockey program in Massachusetts need a new president? Well, someone on the board knows someone. There hasn't been any true outreach, and it works, well, *kinda* OK, right?

"The status quo is strong," said Jackson. "We don't do a lot of outreach, so we don't find the people who will be transformative thinkers. The culture has been created of how people stay within USA Hockey, and how people rise up to be leaders in USA Hockey."

Sheldon Kennedy was sexually abused by predator and coach Graham James when he played junior hockey for the Swift Current Broncos. He went on to play in the NHL, but his greatest impact has been as a champion for marginalized athletes. He's the cofounder of the Respect Group, which delivers programming to coaches and teams in a wide variety of sports, aimed at making arenas, courts, and fields safer and more inclusive.

Kennedy said that hockey must remain vigilant about its culture.

"In my opinion, it's not just hockey culture, it's just culture in general," he said. "But culture, I believe, is an ongoing practice and skill. If we don't prioritize it and practice it and pay attention to it within any organization, or within our ecosystem of friends and family, it doesn't exist. To me, it's a practiced skill. Psychological safety is a practiced skill. We can't just build culture on a hope and a prayer to trade. We need to prioritize and strategize around how we are going to build culture.

"What does that look like? What's our strategy around building a strong culture, and what's important to building a strong culture? What are the benefits of a strong culture? We know that most winning organizations, not just in hockey but in general, the most successful companies, have strong cultures. They pay attention to that. This doesn't mean 'we're going to win forever!' This means, how are we going to treat people with respect? How are we going to step up and step in when we see somebody out of line? How do we address this? How do we come forward? How do we discuss difficult issues?"

THE 22ND CENTURY

So where is hockey a hundred years from now?

There are lots of people who are trying to change the culture of the game at hyper-local and regional levels. There are charities that help kids in need get into the game. There are numbers of organizations that offer specialized programming that make racialized hockey fans and players feel more welcome in the game.

The Little Native Hockey League celebrated its fiftieth anniversary in 2024. The tournament, held annually in Markham, Ontario, brings together First Nations from across Canada's most populous province. Its hall of fame includes former NHL fifty-goal scorer Jonathan Cheechoo and ex-NHL coach Ted Nolan. The Chief Thunderstick tournament, founded by the late Fred Sasakamoose, brings together Indigenous teams from across Canada. In 2024, more than forty teams registered for the tournament.

The Black Girl Hockey Club, formed in 2018 by La Sierra University's Renee Hess, has expanded into Canada. It offers education programs, scholarship opportunities, and education, all aimed at attracting girls of color to the game and making them feel more welcome once they get there. It offers scholarships named for some of the Black pioneers in women's hockey—Hall of Famer Angela James, Bernice Carnegie, Saroya Tinker, and Kia Nurse, to name a few.

Davis pointed to a recent project the NHL undertook with the Black Girl Hockey Club. The Washington Capitals hosted a weekend for a hundred families, and the event combined hockey with a tour of the Smithsonian's National Museum of African American History and Culture.

These programs, and others that aren't mentioned in this book, deserve to be saluted.

But in the middle of it all is the monolith we know as The Culture. It is heavy. It is not easily moved. And there's the other side to this: it's wonderful that we have so many emerging programs that target families of color; but we have to make sure there's a chance for athletes to not get trapped, either—if we feel good because the Black or Indigenous or South Asian kids get one block of ice time a week where they play against one another, with no hope of breaking down the barriers that exist in rep teams and the mainstream hockey organizations, then we're not really tearing down any walls.

While programs from retail giants and grassroots organizations are great, the fact that they exist is a reminder that, for many Americans and Canadians, hockey is a no-go without some kind of help. In its 2022–23 annual report, Hockey Canada reported that 7,479 kids participated in the NHL/NHLPA First Shift program, where, for six weeks, kids get new hockey gear and try the sport for the first time. According to the Hockey Canada report, First Shift "is designed to ensure an accessible, affordable, safe and fun experience for new-to-hockey families."

The existence of so many charitable efforts such as First Shift only proves that the status quo is not equitable. If hockey was indeed equitable, parents wouldn't need to find help just to get their kids a decent stick and a pair of skates.

Charities make societies feel good about themselves. But do we ever consider the deeper questions: Why do they exist in the first place? Why are we creating so many gaps that have to be covered by special efforts? What if MADD was forced to disband because there were no longer impaired drivers on our streets? What if GoFundMe campaigns for sick or injured people were no longer needed because our systems ensured that becoming ill didn't mean you could incur bills or lose your job?

Those are the same questions we need to ask about hockey. Why do so many charitable efforts need to be made to get kids into the game? Why have we created a sport with so many systemic cultural and financial barriers?

The fewer kids who play the game will lead to a shrinking fan base. That's basic economics.

How do we get there? How do we convince parents that their nine- and ten-year-olds don't need to travel for tournaments or wield sticks that cost hundreds of dollars each? How do we make sure coaches are educated not just about the latest drills and strategies but about the racialized history of the game? How do we make the community rink a truly shared space?

Crystal M. Fleming tells us that Americans need to look for a new ideal—that looking back fondly at the oh-so-noble Founding Fathers isn't noble at all. "In order to envision and build a more just society, we will have to collectively recognize the foundational immorality of the Founding Fathers and commit to creating a world better than the one they conceived."[4]

It's a big statement, but the point is well taken. Why look to white men who kept slaves? Why look to men who wanted to keep voting rights exclusively in the hands of white landowners? Is this the democratic ideal?

Fleming's pronunciation can be applied to long-standing institutions, too. Do we need to rely on hockey's old-school unwritten "culture"? Do we allow too much of the sport's history to inform the thinking of the present? Do we look at hockey's culture and say, we need to build a "just" sport—and to do that means burning down what's come before?

Or is it not about changing what the term "the culture" means in hockey?

"The word 'culture' means different things to different people," said USA Hockey's Jackson. "So, now, we are undergoing serious self-examination of what 'culture' meant decades ago, what it means now, and what it will mean in the future."

The work has begun. But we have to admit to ourselves that we're very early in this journey.

Davis admits that. She knows that the real barometer of how hockey is doing will come when changemakers like her, Jackson, and Chaudhry have stepped aside. If the torch is picked up by those who come after, "that tells me we are making the kind of change that is sustainable, that is now going to be part of the infrastructure and the DNA of the sport—so, when I leave, all of this doesn't leave with me."

The first recorded hockey game with formal rules was played at Montreal's McGill University on March 3, 1875. But we know hockey existed before that, in some forms. There are paintings from the early 1800s that depict kids wielding sticks, skating on frozen ponds. So far, hockey historians have discounted claims that the Arctic community of Deline, Northwest Territories, hosted hockey games in the 1820s. Sir John Franklin, during his voyages to find the Northwest Passage, diarized that his crew played "hockey on ice" and skated. But because the entries about skating and hockey aren't linked, historians have disregarded the claim—the men could have been skating, then playing what Franklin called "hockey" without blades on their feet.

No matter where you believe hockey was born, or if you even care, we've seen the game evolve over the years. In its early days, it was played with seven players a side, and games were split into two halves. Players weren't allowed to raise the puck off the ice.

We didn't allow the game to remain that way. It got faster. Better. Tougher.

The game itself is an incredible mix of speed and power. It is a game that rewards toughness and skill equally. And it deserves a lot better than how we've treated it.

STICK TAPS

I **'VE OFTEN WONDERED** if I could simply write whatever I wanted in the acknowledgments section, knowing most of the readers have closed the book by now—or maybe, just maybe, flung it across the room.

But for those of you sticking around—I'd like to thank you, first and foremost. We live in a time where the act of reading, especially when it comes to topics of race and the need for change, is an act of rebellion.

At the end of every NHL game, the Three Stars are announced. There are far more than three stars who helped make this book possible.

Thanks go out to Joanna Green at Beacon Press, and my agent, Wayne Arthurson at The Rights Factory, for their belief in this project. I thank you for your passion.

My wife, Noelle, was patient with me to a fault. It's not easy to live with a writer; I hog the kitchen table, it's filled with notes and books, and when I open my laptop, I come precariously close to spilling my coffee.

To our kids, Tate and Nico, thanks for putting up with dad trying to sneak work in while we were on our sports road trips. The two of you are the world to your mother and me.

To Trudy Callaghan, publisher of *Edify* magazine, thanks to allowing me the space and time to indulge myself in this passion project.

I thank Jay Ball for his enthusiastic support. And to my friend, Jennifer Walton, for being my trusted beta reader.

Thank you to the Canada Council of the Arts for providing grant support for this project.

My wife works for the Edmonton Public Library; the library was an invaluable resource as I researched this project. When I walked into the

Woodcroft branch, I'd see posters encouraging readers to embrace banned books. That's the kind of library I'm proud to have in the city in which I live. We need to embrace and fund libraries—they promote literacy, a sense of community, and are great gathering places, where knowledge is offered without judgment.

Find a list of books that are banned by your local government or school board. Read one. Celebrate the fact that you can be offended.

Through the process of researching this project, I've read so many books and articles by myriad thoughtful writers, which rightly point out that white people often react defensively when they are confronted with how they've benefited from racism, or how there are still so many structures that exist in our modern society which put minority groups at a disadvantage.

There have been a lot of people in hockey—owners, general managers, players, minor-hockey coaches, and officials—who have been guilty of being defensive, of stalling change for the simple reason—*that's the way it's always been.*

Since I started writing it, I have seen this book as a tough-love letter to the game. My feelings on this have only grown stronger as I come to the end of this book. I may be turning off my laptop, this book might be closing, but the journey is only beginning.

Hockey, I certainly can't quit you, but, come on, there are things that really have to change. It's taken me a long time to recognize that good enough in this sport simply isn't good enough. I hope others can see it, too.

READING LIST

Angie Abdou. *Home Ice: Reflections of a Reluctant Hockey Mom*. Toronto: ECW Press, 2018.

Akim Aliu and Greg Anderson Elysee. *Dreamer: A Graphic Novel Memoir*. Illustrated by Karen De La Vega. New York: Graphix, 2023.

Eliza Barlow. "The Parenting Crunch." *Avenue Edmonton*, February 2020, pp. 40–43.

Howard Bryant. *Full Dissidence: Notes from an Uneven Playing Field*. Boston: Beacon Press, 2020.

Dan Bylsma and Jay Bylsma. *So Your Son Wants to Play in the NHL?* Toronto: McClelland & Stewart, 1998.

Ken Campbell and Jim Parcels. *Selling the Dream: How Hockey Parents and Their Kids Are Paying the Price for Our National Obsession*. Toronto: Viking, 2013.

Herb Carnegie and Bernice Carnegie. *A Fly in a Pail of Milk: The Herb Carnegie Story*. Toronto: ECW Press, 2019.

Robin DiAngelo. *White Fragility: Why It's So Hard for White People to Talk About Racism*. Boston: Beacon Press, 2018.

Crystal M. Fleming. *How to Be Less Stupid About Race: On Racism, White Supremacy, and the Racial Divide*. Boston: Beacon Press, 2018.

George Fosty and Darril Fosty. *George & Darril Fosty's Black Ice: The Lost History of the Colored Hockey League of the Maritimes, 1895–1925*. Halifax: Nimbus Publishing, 2017.

Victor Hedman. "How We Play Hockey in Sweden." *Players' Tribune*, February 10, 2016. https://www.theplayerstribune.com/articles/victor-hedman-lightning-sweden-hockey.

Mark Hyman. *Until It Hurts: America's Obsession with Youth Sports and How It Harms Our Kids*. Boston: Beacon Press, 2010.

Valmore James and John Gallagher. *Black Ice: The Val James Story*. Toronto: ECW Press, 2015.

Perry King. *Rebound: Sports, Community and the Inclusive City*. Toronto: Coach House Books, 2021.

Jeff Z. Klein and Karl-Eric Reif. *The Death of Hockey; or How a Bunch of Guys with Too Much Money and Too Little Sense Are Killing the Greatest Game on Earth*. Toronto: Macmillan Canada, 1998.

John Manasso. *A Season of Loss, a Lifetime of Forgiveness: The Dan Snyder and Dany Heatley Story*. Toronto: ECW Press, 2005.

Evan F. Moore. "'Let's Take This as an Opportunity': How Youth Hockey Is Curbing Racism." *Global Sport Matters*, May 3, 2022. https://globalsportmat ters.com/youth/2022/05/03/how-youth-hockey-curbing-racism-nhl/.

Evan F. Moore and Jashvina Shah. *Game Misconduct: Hockey's Toxic Culture and How to Fix It*. Chicago: Triumph, 2021.

Nicole Mortillaro. *Willie O'Ree: The Story of the First Black Player in the NHL*. Toronto: James Lorimer & Co., 2012.

Susan Neiman. *Left Is Not Woke*. Cambridge: Polity Press, 2023.

Lorna Schultz Nicholson. *Amazing Hockey Stories: P. K. Subban*. Toronto: Scholastic Canada, 2019.

Ted Nolan and Meg Masters. *Life in Two Worlds: A Coach's Journey from the Reserve to the NHL and Back*. Toronto: Viking Canada, 2023.

Willie O'Ree and Michael McKinley. *Willie: The Game-Changing Story of the NHL's First Black Player*. Toronto: Viking Canada, 2020.

Sunaya Sapurji. "Grassroots to Gold: Sweden Uses Innovative Thinking to Tackle Development, Challenges." *The Athletic*, November 30, 2017. https://the athletic.com/147362/2017/11/30/grassroots-to-gold-sweden-uses-innovative -thinking-to-tackle-development-challenges/.

Fred Sasakamoose. *Call Me Indian: From the Trauma of Residential School to Becoming the NHL's First Treaty Indigenous Player*. Toronto: Viking Canada, 2021.

Erin Silver. *Proud to Play: Canadian LGBTQ+ Athletes Who Made History*. Toronto: James Lorimer & Co., 2021.

Wayne Simmonds. "Wayne's Road Hockey Warriors." In *Everyday Hockey Heroes: Inspiring Stories On and Off the Ice*. Edited by Bob McKenzie and Jim Lang. Toronto: Simon & Schuster Canada, 2018, pp. 1–10.

Harnarayan Singh. "A Boy with a Dream." In *Everyday Hockey Heroes: Inspiring Stories On and Off the Ice*. Edited by Bob McKenzie and Jim Lang. Simon & Schuster Canada, 2018, pp. 69–88.

Karl Subban and Scott Colby. *How We Did It: The Subban Plan for Success in Hockey, School and Life*. Toronto: Random House Canada, 2017.

Courtney Szto. *Changing on the Fly: Hockey Through the Voices of South Asian Canadians*. New Brunswick, NJ: Rutgers University Press, 2021.

Courtney Szto, Sam McKegney, Mike Auksi, and Bob Dawson. *Policy Paper for Anti-Racism in Canadian Hockey*, 2019. https://hockeyinsociety.files.wordpress .com/2020/02/policypaper_anti-racisminhockey_execsummary_final.pdf.

FILM

Black Ice. Directed by Hubert Davis. Elevation Pictures, 2022.

INTERVIEWS AND MEDIA AVAILABILITIES

Tim Adams, interviewed February 2022.

Akim Aliu, interviewed October 2022 at Hockey Diversity Alliance event.

Arshdeep Bains, interviewed November 2022.

Ethan Bear, from recorded NHL press conferences.

Bernice Carnegie, interviewed October 2022 at Hockey Diversity Alliance event.

Anson Carter, interviewed via Zoom, October 2023.

Irfan Chaudhry, interviewed September 2023.

Dan Cote-Rosen, interviewed via Zoom, February 2024.

Kim Davis, interviewed via Zoom, October 2023.

Matt Dumba, interviewed via Zoom, December 2022.

Mattias Ekholm, media availability, March 2024.

Jarome Iginla, from Hockey Hall of Fame induction appearance, November 2021.

Stephanie Jackson, telephone interview, March 2024.

Dakota Joshua, from recorded NHL press conferences.

Nazem Kadri, from recorded NHL press conferences.

Evander Kane, media conferences, including January 2022 signing with Edmonton Oilers.

Sheldon Kennedy, media availability, July 2024.

Mark Fraser, interviewed October 2022 at Hockey Diversity Alliance event.

Georges Laraque, interviewed October 2022.

Connor McDavid, media availability, March 2024.

Pete Nguyen, interviewed via Zoom, February 2024.

Darnell Nurse, interview, February 2022; portions appear in *Edify* magazine, April
2022.

Bill Peters, press conference, August 2023.

Jason Robertson, media availability, November 2022.

Sonny Sekhon, interviewed August 2023.

P. K. Subban, interviewed via Zoom, October 2023.

Saroya Tinker, interviewed October 2022 at Hockey Diversity Alliance event.

Lali Toor, interviewed August 2022 and November 2023.

John Tortorella, from recorded NHL press conferences.

Zach Whitecloud, interviewed November 2022 and via phone, February 2023.

NOTES

ONE: THE WAY FORWARD

1. John Rosengren, "Alum Mike Grier Is Hockey's First Black General Manager," *Bostonia*, February 14, 2023, https://www.bu.edu/articles/2023/alum-mike-grier-is-hockeys-first-black-general-manager/.

2. Jason Newland, "NHL Witnessing a Decline in Stanley Cup Final Viewership," *Hockey News*, June 11, 2023, https://thehockeynews.com/nhl/columbus-blue-jackets/news/nhl-witnessing-a-decline-in-stanley-cup-final-viewership.

3. "NHL, Diamond Reach Broadcast Deal for 11 Teams," *Sports Business Journal*, December 21, 2023, https://www.sportsbusinessjournal.com/Articles/2023/12/21/nhl-diamond-sports-group-agreement-broadcast-11-teams.aspx.

4. Evan F. Moore and Jashvina Shah, *Game Misconduct: Hockey's Toxic Culture and How to Fix It* (Chicago: Triumph, 2021), 72.

5. Richard Raycraft, "Hockey Canada Paid Out $8.9-Million in Sexual Abuse Settlements Since 1989," CBC News, July 27, 2022, https://www.cbc.ca/news/politics/hockey-canada-house-of-commons-committee-1.6533439.

TWO: WHERE IT'S BEEN

1. Kevin Bissett, "Momentum Growing in Effort to Get Willie O'Ree into Hockey Hall of Fame," *National Post*, March 3, 2018, https://nationalpost.com/pmn/sports-pmn/hockey-sports-pmn/momentum-growing-in-effort-to-get-willie-oree-into-hockey-hall-of-fame-2.

2. Matt Kelly, "The 37 Negro Leagues Legends in the HOF," MLB.com, January 31, 2022, https://www.mlb.com/news/negro-leaguers-in-the-national-baseball-hall-of-fame.

3. George Fosty and Darril Fosty, *George & Darril Fosty's Black Ice: The Lost History of the Colored Hockey League of the Maritimes, 1895–1925* (Halifax: Nimbus Publishing, 2017), 6–7.

4. Willie O'Ree and Michael McKinley, *Willie: The Game-Changing Story of the NHL's First Black Player* (Toronto: Viking Canada, 2020), 1.

5. Fosty and Fosty, *George & Darril Fosty's Black Ice*, 59.

6. Fosty and Fosty, *George & Darril Fosty's Black Ice*, 90.

7. Avry Lewis McDougall, "Changing the Hall," Avryssports.com, June 24, 2024, https://avrysports.com/f/changing-the-hall.

8. Susan Neiman, *Left Is Not Woke* (Cambridge: Polity Press, 2023), 125.

9. O'Ree and McKinley, *Willie*, 40.

10. Mac Engel, "For O'Ree, a Fight All the Way," *Washington Post*, March 2, 2003, https://www.washingtonpost.com/archive/sports/2003/03/02/for-oree -a-fight-all-the-way/a8b9d2d9–6ae6–4098-a20e-7e2e45398a14/.

11. Nicole Mortillaro, *Willie O'Ree: The Story of the First Black Player in the NHL* (Toronto: James Lorimer & Co., 2012), 99.

12. Ben Raby, "Against the Odds: Remembering Mike Marson's Career with the Caps," NHL.com/Capitals, February 25, 2019, https://www.nhl.com/capitals /news/against-the-odds-remembering-mike-marsons-career-with-the-caps /c-305201080.

13. Valmore James and John Gallagher, *Black Ice: The Val James Story* (Toronto: ECW Press, 2015).

14. Robin DiAngelo, *White Fragility: Why It's So Hard for White People to Talk About Racism* (Boston: Beacon Press, 2018), 26.

15. Herb Carnegie and Bernice Carnegie, *A Fly in a Pail of Milk: The Herb Carnegie Story* (Toronto: ECW Press, 2019), 40–41.

16. Steven Sandor, *The Battle of Alberta: A Century of Hockey's Greatest Rivalry* (Victoria, BC: Heritage House, 2005), 66.

17. Miles Morrisseau, "Canada's Forgotten Olympian: Kenneth Moore," *Indian Country Today*, February 15, 2022, https://ictnews.org/news/canadas -forgotten-olympian-kenneth-moore.

18. Grow the Game Summit, "Keynote: Anti-Racism in Canadian Hockey," available at https://www.youtube.com/watch?v=TLRcU9N8X24, accessed January 4, 2024.

19. Stephanie Coratti, "Show Them Seaside: Seaside Hockey Celebrates Community and Growth," GTHLCanada.com, February 20, 2023, https:// gthlcanada.com/article/show-them-seaside-seaside-hockey-celebrates-community -growth.

20. Robert L. McDougall, "Duncan Campbell Scott," *The Canadian Encyclopedia*, August 11, 2008, https://www.thecanadianencyclopedia.ca/en/article/duncan -campbell-scott.

21. Fred Sasakamoose, *Call Me Indian: From the Trauma of Residential School to Becoming the NHL's First Treaty Indigenous Player* (Toronto: Viking Canada, 2021), 40–41.

22. Sasakamoose, *Call Me Indian*, 177.

23. "Sports and Reconciliation," Crown-Indigenous Relations and Northern Affairs Canada, Government of Canada, last modified June 26, 2024, https://www .rcaanc-cirnac.gc.ca/eng/1524505883755/1557512006268.

THREE: WHERE WE ARE

1. Gare Joyce, "The Full Cost," Sportsnet.ca, https://www.sportsnet.ca/hockey/nhl/akim-aliu-hockey-hazing-big-read/, retrieved April 15, 2023.

2. "Akim Aliu," *Elite Prospects*, https://www.eliteprospects.com/player/11116/akim-aliu, retrieved April 15, 2013.

3. Gare Joyce, "The Full Cost," Sportsnet.ca, https://www.sportsnet.ca/hockey/nhl/akim-aliu-hockey-hazing-big-read/, retrieved April 15, 2023.

4. Mouhamad Rachini. "Akim Aliu Faces Off Against Hockey's Harsh Realities in Graphic Memoir for Kids," CBC.ca, February 11, 2023, https://www.cbc.ca/radio/sunday/akim-aliu-hockey-graphic-memoir-1.6740823.

5. Akim Aliu and Greg Anderson Elysee, *Dreamer: A Graphic Novel Memoir*, illustrated by Karen De La Vega (New York: Graphix, 2023), 101.

6. Steven Sandor, "Behind the Bench," *Home Ice* (magazine), January 1, 2015, 16.

7. Jenna West, "Ex-Hurricane Michal Jordán Accuses Bill Peters of Abuse," *Sports Illustrated*, November 26, 2019, https://www.si.com/nhl/2019/11/26/bill-peters-physical-abuse-allegations-michal-jordan-hurricanes.

8. "We Are Sport—Diversity and Leadership Panel Discussion," Black Girl Hockey Club, August 28, 2020, https://blackgirlhockeyclub.org/2020/08/28/we-are-sport-diversity-and-leadership-panel-discussion/.

9. "CHL Statement on Racial Equality," CHL, June 1, 2020, https://chl.ca/article/chl-statement-on-racial-equality/.

10. Ian Kennedy, "Flint Firebirds' President of Hockey Ops Expelled from OHL," *Hockey News*, March 10, 2022, https://thehockeynews.com/news/flint-firebirds-president-of-hockey-ops-expelled-from-ohl.

11. Grow the Game Summit, "Keynote: Anti-Racism in Canadian Hockey," https://www.youtube.com/watch?v=TLRcU9N8X24, accessed Jan. 4, 2024.

12. Valmore James and John Gallagher, *Black Ice: The Val James Story* (Toronto: ECW Press, 2015), 49.

13. Courtney Szto, *Changing on the Fly: Hockey Through the Voices of South Asian Canadians* (New Brunswick, NJ: Rutgers University Press, 2021), 1.

14. "Los Angeles Kings Pick Akil Thomas Recounts Journey as Black Hockey Player," NBC Sports, October 27, 2020, https://nhl.nbcsports.com/tag/akil-thomas/.

15. Cole Schisler, "Coquitlam Family Calls for Accountability After Claims of Racism, Assault in Minor Hockey," *CityNews Vancouver*, December 5, 2022, https://vancouver.citynews.ca/2022/12/05/coquitlam-hockey-racism-assault/.

16. Jamie Strashin, "Toronto Hockey League Investigating Teen's Allegation of Racial Slur During Game," CBC.ca, October 7, 2022, https://www.cbc.ca/sports/hockey/hockey-racial-slur-toronto-gthl-1.6609450.

17. Natalie Van Rooy, "Gatineau Minor Hockey Player Speaks Out About Racist Incidents," CTVNews.ca (Ottawa), March 31, 2022, https://ottawa.ctvnews.ca/gatineau-minor-hockey-player-speaks-out-about-racist-incidents-1.5843517.

18. "Game Misconduct: Canadians May Love Their Hockey, but They Also See Serious Problems with Its Culture," Angus Reid Institute, May 5, 2021, https://angusreid.org/hockey-culture/.

19. Sidhartha Banerjee, "5 P.E.I. Minor Hockey Players Suspended 25 Games over Racial Slurs Toward N.S. Player," GlobalNews.ca, February 11, 2022, https://globalnews.ca/news/8612851/pei-minor-hockey-players-suspended-racial-slurs/.

20. Black Girl Hockey Club, "A Juneteenth Discussion with Black Girl Hockey Club," June 22, 2020, https://blackgirlhockeyclub.org/2020/06/22/a-junteenth-discussion-with-black-girl-hockey-club/.

21. Uninterrupted with EA Sports, "How Indigenous NHL Defenseman Ethan Bear Turned Racism & Hate into a Chance to Teach," February 22, 2022, https://www.youtube.com/watch?v=WwCfJHiB0IU.

22. Greg Wyshynski, "John Tortorella Reverses Hardline Stance on Kneeling," ESPN.com, June 10, 2020, https://www.espn.com/nhl/story/_/id/29293541/john-tortorella-reverses-hardline-stance-kneeling.

23. Ryan S. Clark, "NHL Commissioner Bettman: No More Specialty Sweaters During Warmups," ESPN.com, June 22, 2023, https://www.espn.co.uk/nhl/story/_/id/37901150/nhl-commissioner-no-more-specialty-sweaters-warmups.

FOUR: THE MONEY BARRIER

1. "Neighbourhood Profile: Flemingdon Park," City of Toronto, 2016, https://www.toronto.ca/ext/sdfa/Neighbourhood%20Profiles/pdf/2016/pdf1/cpa44.pdf; "Neighbourhood Profile: Malvern," City of Toronto, 2016, https://www.toronto.ca/ext/sdfa/Neighbourhood%20Profiles/pdf/2016/pdf1/cpa132.pdf.

2. Ken Campbell and Jim Parcels, *Selling the Dream: How Hockey Parents and Their Kids Are Paying the Price for Our National Obsession* (Toronto: Viking, 2013), 139.

3. "Jarome Iginla on His Journey, George Floyd and the Need for Change," Sportsnet.ca, June 4, 2020, https://www.sportsnet.ca/hockey/nhl/iginla-felt-fortunate-support-others-hockey-journey/.

4. Minnesota Hockey, "Choosing the Right Hockey Stick," Sports Engine, August 26, 2019, https://www.minnesotahockey.org/news_article/show/1043906.

5. Campbell and Parcels, *Selling the Dream*, 141.

6. Karl Subban and Scott Colby, *How We Did It: The Subban Plan for Success in Hockey, School and Life* (Toronto: Random House Canada, 2017), 5.

7. Victor Hedman, "How We Play Hockey in Sweden," *Players' Tribune*, February 10, 2016, https://www.theplayerstribune.com/articles/victor-hedman-lightning-sweden-hockey.

8. Steven Sandor, "A Hockey Factory," *Blaze*, January 20, 2003, 51.

9. Dan Bylsma and Jay Bylsma, *So Your Son Wants to Play in the NHL?* (Toronto: McClelland & Stewart, 1998), 25.

10. Grow the Game Summit, "Keynote: Anti-Racism in Canadian Hockey," https://www.youtube.com/watch?v=TLRcU9N8X24, accessed January 4, 2024.

FIVE: YOU MADE IT, NOW FOLLOW THE STEREOTYPE, PLEASE

1. Rachel Alexander, "Carter Takes His Best Shot," *Washington Post*, September 20, 1996, https://www.washingtonpost.com/archive/sports/1996/09/20/carter -takes-his-best-shot/2c6110cb-c1ee-4b72–8c77-b1c7fd10504e/.

2. Valmore James and John Gallagher, *Black Ice: The Val James Story* (Toronto: ECW Press, 2015), 111.

3. Fred Sasakamoose, *Call Me Indian: From the Trauma of Residential School to Becoming the NHL's First Treaty Indigenous Player* (Toronto: Viking Canada, 2021), 76–77.

4. Herb Carnegie and Bernice Carnegie, *A Fly in a Pail of Milk: The Herb Carnegie Story* (Toronto: ECW Press, 2019), 40–41.

5. Courtney Szto, *Changing on the Fly: Hockey Through the Voices of South Asian Canadians* (New Brunswick, NJ: Rutgers University Press, 2021), 58.

6. Howard Bryant, *Full Dissidence: Notes from an Uneven Playing Field* (Boston: Beacon Press, 2020), 81.

7. Bryant, *Full Dissidence*, 97.

SIX: GUILTY OF BEING WHITE

1. Steven Sandor, "Kane Asks Fans to Keep Open Mind as Controversial Forward Joins Oilers," CBC.ca, January 28, 2022, https://www.cbc.ca/sports/hockey /nhl/nhl-edmonton-oilers-evander-kane-presser-1.6331251.

2. Steven Sandor, "Jagr on Ice," *Prague Post*, April 10, 2003.

3. "NHL's MacTavish Is Released After Serving One Year in Jail," *Los Angeles Times*, May 14, 1985, https://www.latimes.com/archives/la-xpm-1985–05–14-sp -19126-story.html.

4. "Dany Heatley Avoids Jail Time," CBC.ca, February 4, 2005, https://www .cbc.ca/sports/hockey/dany-heatley-avoids-jail-time-1.556751.

5. Grow the Game Summit, "Unconscious Bias and Its Impact on Sports," available at https://www.youtube.com/watch?v=fMuAoOUd2J4&t=2275s, accessed January 2, 2024.

6. Crystal M. Fleming, *How to Be Less Stupid About Race: On Racism, White Supremacy, and the Racial Divide* (Boston: Beacon Press, 2018), 47.

7. Doug Millroy, "How Long Does Vanbiesbrouck Have to Pay for a Racial Slur?" *Sault This Week*, January 16, 2024, https://www.saultthisweek.com/opinion /columnists/how-long-does-vanbiesbrouck-have-to-pay-for-a-racial-slur.

8. James Hopkin, "'False and Inflammatory': Soo Greyhounds Deny Claims Made by Former Goalie," Sudbury.com, April 12, 2024, https://www.sudbury.com /beyond-local/false-and-inflammatory-soo-greyhounds-deny-claims-made-by -former-goalie-8590528.

SEVEN: THE CULTURE OF SILENCE

1. Zach Whitecloud (@zachwhitecloud), "Reconciliation requires truth, sincerity, and accountability for our words and actions," Instagram post, September 30, 2022, https://www.instagram.com/p/CjJZdT-PA_G/.

2. Fred Sasakamoose, *Call Me Indian: From the Trauma of Residential School to Becoming the NHL's First Treaty Indigenous Player* (Toronto: Viking Canada, 2021), 88.

3. Ted Nolan and Meg Masters, *Life in Two Worlds: A Coach's Journey from the Reserve to the NHL and Back* (Toronto: Viking Canada, 2023), 241.

4. Willie O'Ree and Michael McKinley, *Willie: The Game-Changing Story of the NHL's First Black Player* (Toronto: Viking Canada, 2020), 142.

5. Robin DiAngelo, *White Fragility: Why It's So Hard for White People to Talk About Racism* (Boston: Beacon Press, 2018), 127.

6. ESPN and FiveThirtyEight, "Election 2020: Inside the Political Donation History of Wealthy Sports Owners," ESPN.com, October 28, 2020, https://www.espn.com/nba/story/_/id/30155186/election-2020-political-donation-history-wealthy-sports-owners.

7. Ed Malyon, "Arsenal Owner Stan Kroenke Donated $1 Million to Donald Trump's Inauguration Fund," *Independent*, April 19, 2017, https://www.independent.co.uk/sport/football/premier-league/arsenal-stan-kroenke-donated-1billion-donald-trump-a7691536.html.

8. Hadas Gold, "Canadian Billionaire's Company Buys Laura Ingraham's Site LifeZette," *CNN Business*, January 30, 2018, https://money.cnn.com/2018/01/30/media/daryl-katz-laura-ingraham-lifezette/index.html.

9. Howard Bryant, *Full Dissidence: Notes from an Uneven Playing Field* (Boston: Beacon Press, 2020), 24.

10. Joshua Clipperton, "NHL Postpones Thursday, Friday Games After Shooting of Jacob Blake," *Winnipeg Free Press*, August 27, 2020, https://www.winnipegfreepress.com/breakingnews/2020/08/27/hockey-diversity-alliance-asks-nhl-to-suspend-thursdays-playoff-games.

CHAPTER EIGHT: WHERE WILL WE BE A CENTURY FROM NOW?

1. Robin DiAngelo, *White Fragility: Why It's So Hard for White People to Talk About Racism* (Boston: Beacon Press, 2018), xii.

2. Courtney Szto, *Changing on the Fly: Hockey Through the Voices of South Asian Canadians* (New Brunswick, NJ: Rutgers University Press, 2021), 27.

3. Ian Mendes, "Snoop Dogg on Bid to Buy the Ottawa Senators; 'This Ain't No Joke,'" *The Athletic*, May 4, 2023, https://theathletic.com/4485487/2023/05/04/snoop-dogg-ottawa-senators-interview/.

4. Crystal M. Fleming, *How to Be Less Stupid About Race: On Racism, White Supremacy, and the Racial Divide* (Boston: Beacon Press, 2018), 46–47.

INDEX